1968

This book may be kept

FOURT

A fine will be char

ENGLISH
AND THE
DISADVANTAGED

edited by

EDWARD R. FAGAN

Professor of Education
The Pennsylvania State University

INTERNATIONAL TEXTBOOK COMPANY
Scranton, Pennsylvania

ACKNOWLEDGMENTS

The editor wishes to thank the following authors and publishers for permission to reprint, in amended form, the contents of articles which first appeared in the following publications, under the titles listed below.

"English for What?" from the December 1965 *Teachers College Record*, by Charles Weingartner. Used by permission of Teachers College, Columbia University.

"English in Relation to Social Needs" from the April 1965 *Journal of General Education*, by William M. Dallam. Used by permission of the Pennsylvania State University Press.

"The English Teacher: A Major Cause of School Drop-outs," from the October 1965 *English Journal*, by Robert J. Graham. Used by permission of the National Council of Teachers of English.

The editor also wishes to thank his wife, Rosemarie (Niro) Fagan, and his family, Patricia, Timothy, Paul, Barry, Christopher, and Corrine, for their patience, understanding, and willingness to be "disadvantaged" while work on the manuscript was in progress.

EDWARD R. FAGAN

CONTRIBUTORS

WILLIAM M. DALLAM, Department of Public Instruction, Commonwealth of Pennsylvania, was national co-ordinator for the compilation of materials for teaching English to the disadvantaged and the director of a workshop organized for that purpose at the National Council of Teachers of English Annual Convention held in Cleveland, Ohio in November 1964.

ANITA E. DUNN, Associate Professor of English Education, State University of New York at Albany, has taught English to disadvantaged youth in Waukesha and Madison, Wisconsin, in Hawaii, and in Albany, New York; she is co-author (1953) and editor (1964) of *Fare for The Reluctant Reader*.

EDWARD R. FAGAN, Professor of Education, The Pennsylvania State University, has taught English to disadvantaged youth in Waukesha and Madison, Wisconsin and in Albany, New York; he directed the NDEA, Title XI, Summer 1965, Institute for Teachers and Supervisors of Disadvantaged Youth in English and Reading at the University.

ROBERT J. GRAHAM, Assistant Professor of English and Education, The Pennsylvania State University, University Park, Pennsylvania, has taught disadvantaged youth in urban and rural New Jersey and Pennsylvania; the materials he has developed have been utilized in national periodicals and NDEA workshops.

THEODORA R. GRAHAM, Instructor in English, The Pennsylvania State University, developed curriculum guides and conducted NDEA workshop programs in linguistics and composition; she has taught English to disadvantaged youth in junior and senior high schools in New Jersey.

CLEMENS L. HALLMAN, Associate Director, Indiana Language Program, Indiana University, has served as consultant on foreign languages to the University of Notre Dame, the U.S. Office of Education, and the Indiana State Education Department; he has had experience with language problems of disadvantaged youth.

HELEN M. KOCH, Teacher of English, Indiana High School, Indiana, Pennsylvania, has taught English to disadvantaged students over a number of years and has been the recipient of many awards for excellence in English teaching, among which was her selection as a participant in Pennsylvania State University's NDEA Institute for Teachers and Supervisors of Disadvantaged Youth in English and Reading, Summer 1965.

CHARLES WEINGARTNER, Associate Professor of Education, Queens College, City University of New York, has taught English to disadvantaged youth in Michigan, Virginia, and New York City; he taught the linguistics course at Pennsylvania State University's Summer NDEA Institute for Teachers and Supervisors of Disadvantaged Youth, and he directed Hunter College's institute for the study of educating the disadvantaged, Summer 1966.

JOHN WITHALL, Professor and Head of the Department of Secondary Education, Distinguished Visiting Professor of Educational Psychology, The Pennsylvania State University, has trained Peace Corps teachers for work with the disadvantaged in Pakistan and Africa, and has served as consultant for teachers of disadvantaged in Pennsylvania. He has written widely in professional journals and is the inventor of the Withall Social-Emotional Climate Index, a measuring device for determining effects of classroom climate on learning.

CONTENTS

Introduction

English, for those of us who identify it as our discipline, is a mosaic. Each piece of the discipline—reading, writing, speaking, listening—has a unique identification. Reading, for example, includes vocabulary, comprehension, speed, and word density which makes it identifiable as a skill different from literature yet a part of literature. Such separate but combined aspects of English demand our understanding of bonding principles within the discipline so that we may teach English as a whole rather than as a series of discrete phenomena.

Such *holism* (to use the sociologists' term for this sort of perception) is especially needed for teaching English to disadvantaged students, who are defined throughout this book as those students who meet the federal criteria for such a classification, namely, those who are "socially, culturally, economically, or educationally handicapped youth."[1]* Those who work with disadvantaged students tend to make further distinctions between the urban and rural disadvantaged, but such distinctions do not have to be so finely drawn for this book. While in every city there are third and fourth generation urbanites, there are also growing numbers of immigrants from rural areas who are immersed in value conflicts. These value conflicts are based on the fact that many rural immigrants never accept urban value systems and consider the city a resource for acquiring enough money to return to their rural homes. The attitudes, behaviors, and learning problems such rural students bring to the classroom—whether that classroom is within an urban or rural area—are essentially the same. Our concern for the particular problems these students encounter in English classrooms is the focus of this book.

But the audience for this book is the teacher and prospective teacher of English. Ultimately, the learning any student experiences is the product of some teacher's interpretation, application, and evaluation of a design for learning. In spite of elaborate curriculum guides, "expert" recommendations, and hortatory fiats, the structure and process of learning are the result of an individual teacher's decision to use a particular strategem

* Superscript numbers identify references at the end of each article.

to achieve his school's objectives in the day-to-day English skills needed for survival in contemporary society.

Any teacher of disadvantaged students has few precedents to guide him in his daily struggle to climb a Sinai of doubt. He seldom knows how effective his efforts have been. He is not helped in his efforts by the knowledge that his impact on the junior high school student is virtually nil; research shows that the crucial point for affecting the learning attitudes of the disadvantaged is at the preprimary or primary level. While as high school teachers we cannot refute such findings, we sometimes regard them as unduly pessimistic, particularly when they are based on the assumption that English curricular structures are fixed and inviolate.[2] Besides, as English teachers we cannot write off as *lost* the four million or more disadvantaged students who are *there* in secondary classrooms.

Some hope for these students was implicit in the October 1964 amendments to the National Defense Education Act (NDEA). Under Public Law 85–864, extensions of Title XI coverage to seven additional types of college conducted institutes were permitted, one of which was for "teachers of disadvantaged youth." In 1964, too, our need to concern ourselves with the problem of disadvantaged youth in English was dramatically presented by the then President of the National Council of Teachers of English, Richard Corbin, in a monograph delivered to the Council's membership. Corbin wrote:

> In a most realistic sense, we cannot save the fifty million economically and culturally disadvantaged human beings who are drowning in the sea of our national affluence until we have taught them, beginning in their earliest childhood to speak, to read, and in some measure, to write the words and forms of English that are acceptable to our society. We cannot effectively impart these skills until, through the help of literature, we have struck some spark of self-illumination, a flash of that inner necessary light which informs the human spirit as to what it is and what it can become, and without which we are but vegetables.[3]

Corbin's concern might be attributed to his first-hand contact with urban youth in Harlem via his involvement in the Hunter College Project, but he had expressed similar concerns long before that when he was teaching high school English in Peekskill, New York. That Corbin's eloquence is needed can be inferred from the following examples of "English teaching" as practiced on the disadvantaged: a nineteen year old boy in a Catskill high school having to take ninth-grade English for the fourth time because he failed to pass a ninth-grade Regents examination in the subject; a group of slow-learning eighth graders in Madison, Wisconsin being forced to read aloud (in the stumbling, inarticulate patterns of the non-reader), paragraph by paragraph, student by student, and row by row,

A Tale of Two Cities for an entire eighteen-week semester; a ninth-grade class in the Adirondacks spending six weeks on a "grammar" unit based on diagramming sentences for homework assignments, putting the diagrammed sentences on the board without any teacher feedback as to whether the diagrams were right or wrong, turning in the homework papers which were dumped into the wastebasket while the students watched, and getting more sentences for diagramming for the next day's class.

Fortunately, such teaching is atypical of English programs for the disadvantaged, but the teachers' explanations for the questionable teaching procedures mentioned above were not. In generalized form, typical explanations for what goes on in a disadvantaged classroom are that disadvantaged students are "too stupid to learn" and that teachers' time might better be spent with students who can learn. Given such a rationale, the self-fulfilling prophecies concerning disadvantaged students begin. In operation, the prophecy goes like this: disadvantaged students are too stupid to learn; therefore, one should not make a sincere effort to teach them anything—just keep them busy and quiet; results of schools' end-of-year testing programs show that, indeed, the disadvantaged students did not learn, so the prophecy is fulfilled. Personality effects of such a closed system can readily be imagined: withdrawal, frustration, hostility, and aggression not only against the school but against the whole society which imposes this Procrustean "enlightenment."

More important, the whole sadistic ritual is unnecessary; most states have curricular provisions for special programs for the disadvantaged. Although the term *disadvantaged* may not appear in the curriculum guides and bulletins, the emendation of course structures and time blocks are there for schools who wish to take advantage of them.[4] Frank Brown's description of slow learners' achievements in his book *The Non-Graded High School* implies that curricular changes can be made for disadvantaged students.

While Brown's book is one of many blueprints for curricular designs (others may be found in the Bibliography), we feel that every curriculum is based upon the attitudes, viewpoints, processes, and objectives expressed by its makers. Yet, with the exception of the *objectives* section, the final form of most curricular structures fails to include the makers' attitudinal rationale. We regard such a rationale as crucial to the ultimate success of any curricular design, but as indispensible to curricular blueprints for the English education of disadvantaged students in rural areas.

To that end, our purpose in Part 1 of this book is to describe attitudes and viewpoints concerning the place of English in the daily lives of disadvantaged students. In each of these descriptions we attempt to suggest alternatives to our negative perceptions as well as to provide examples for improving the classroom ambiance of disadvantaged students.

Our purpose in Part 2 of this book is to present some processes and objectives for teaching English to the disadvantaged within arbitrarily circumscribed areas. These areas tend to represent the kinds of learning problems disadvantaged students most often face in an English classroom, that is, "grammar," reading, writing, literature, and media. We recognize the limitations of our selections, but we feel that the principles and concepts identified in each area can be adapted to fit disadvantaged students in local areas—particularly when such adaptations make use of the varied offerings in our Bibliography.

Just two more points should be mentioned. First, we call the reader's attention to the foci used as transition devices before each contributor's article. Each Focus is designed to help the reader to discover those central ideas germane to the article which apply to the English education of disadvantaged students. Second, we ask the reader to remember the mosaic analogy of English as a discipline. Each article, though an entity in itself, should always be examined within the total concept of English as a discipline. We have tried to exemplify this *English-as-mosaic* principle via the last article in this book, "Media and the Disadvantaged." If the mosaic principle seems uncertain and confusing, it simply reflects, on the one hand, the reality of day-to-day living which is confusing, but, on the other, the frustration and the hope of teaching English to the disadvantaged.

REFERENCES

1. U.S. Office of Education. "Bulletin—The National Defense Education Act—Public Law 85-864." Washington, D.C., November 1964, p. 3.

2. Cf. Robert F. Fleming. "Pressure," *The Exchange*. New York: The Metropolitan School Study Council, Teachers College, Columbia University, April 1966, p. 11. One teacher in Fleming's study announced to her class, "I'm sorry. There is no time for questioning today. I must cover the material."

3. Richard Corbin. *Literacy, Literature, and the Disadvantaged*. Champaign, Illinois: National Council of Teachers of English, November 1964, pp. 2–3.

4. *General Curriculum Regulations*. Harrisburg, Pennsylvania: Department of Public Instruction, 1965, p. 12, Section 7-310. "Individualizing Instruction" reports several alternatives to traditional curricular patterns at least one of which (VII) applies to disadvantaged students.

part **1**

ENGLISH—PERCEPTIONS

Focus

Students, bright as well as disadvantaged, develop ways to avoid the subjects and classes that they dislike. Robert E. Sherwood (now a gifted playwright) disliked his English classes. Unusually tall and thin for his age, he made the most of people's concern for his health and used it as an excuse to avoid mundane educational rituals.

John Mason Brown in the *Saturday Review* (August 14, 1965, p. 19) describes Mr. Sherwood's health as it was affected by his formal education—class attendance and similar matters—in a way that has pertinence as a focus for Dr. Weingartner's "English for What?" Mr. Brown writes:

> Sherwood's academic position at Harvard was always uneasy. That his precarious health, the toll of his height, affected his record was incontrovertible. It was the explanation supplied most often by his doctors, his parents and the deans. . . . It appeared to get worse whenever he approached a classroom and better whenever he left one. It made him lackadaisical as a student yet enabled him to be active as an undergraduate. . . . If it contributed to his flunking English A, the most elementary of freshman composition courses, it made it possible for him to be an editor of his Freshman *Redbook* and later to write copiously and well for the *Lampoon,* of which he became president, and also for the Hasty Pudding.

Sherwood's feelings about classroom ambiance are not rare among our great writers in the English language, and his "flunking of English A" is even more common. If those skilled in language do so poorly in formal English classrooms, how much more frustrating is the English ritual faced by disadvantaged students? One possible answer to the not so rhetorical question was made by Francis Keppel, the then Commissioner of Education, in an October 1964 address to the Council for Basic Education in Washington, D.C.

> I think we need to acknowledge, all of us, that the force feeding of academic subjects simply won't work. We need to be more understanding, more flexible and creative if we mean to succeed with the disadvantaged. We need to know much more about how and in what

7

ways to proceed. Here we are only at the beginning. Here we have miles to go before we sleep, before we can assuage our conscience as teachers, as educators in our democracy.

Dr. Weingartner lists first steps in Keppel's suggested "miles"; he also wrestles with Keppel's questions of what, how, and why, and supports his explorations at key points by researched evidence. For changing rituals, "English for What?" is a workable beginning.

English for What?

CHARLES WEINGARTNER

As Montaigne put it (quoting Cicero), "Most commonly the author-itie of them that teach, hinders them that would learne."[1] If anything, this observation is more appropriate today than it was when first made. It is, also, most suitable as a comment on the teaching of English. The demands of the times have affected the teaching of other subjects in high school in ways that have yet to reach English.

When viewed from this perspective, the problems of disadvantaged youth in the English class are not different in kind from those of other students; they are different in degree, and so they are more visible. Might it be that the problem is less with the students than with "English"? Might it be that the form and substance of the subject need to be examined from the point of view of its ostensible purposes and how, or even whether, these purposes are achieved?

Long before "disadvantaged youth" came to be regarded as a special problem, such an examination produced the following report:

> The pupils could parse and construe sentences and point out the various parts of speech with great facility, repeating the rules of grammar applicable in each case, yet were utterly unable to put this theoretical knowledge to any practical use, as they showed when called upon to write an ordinary English letter. . . .[2]

Colonel Francis Wayland Parker, as a member of the school board in Quincy, Massachusetts, wrote this report in 1873. In *Slums and Suburbs*, James Conant notes that Col. Parker went on to develop procedures which were revolutionary and successful. His innovations led John Dewey to refer to him as "the father of progressive education." Today, "progressive education" is an epithet.

At the same time, Francis Keppel, United States Commissioner of Education, notes:

Those who cheer, with good cause, the new problem-solving approach to physics by Dr. Jerrold Zacharias or the new approaches to learning by Dr. Jerome Bruner often fail to realize that they have brilliantly developed what John Dewey conceived a generation ago.[3]

SYMPTOMS AND CAUSES

It is curious that so much of the dialogue about what must be done in English consists of just so much dead rhetoric. It makes about as much sense as talking of new ways to refurbish a steamboat for a trip to the moon.

Since Col. Parker reported what he observed about the lack of relationship between the "naming of the parts" approach to the study of our language and the ability of students to write it, hundreds of studies have been made which simply reaffirmed his conclusions. The *Encyclopedia of Educational Research* reports virtually nothing else. Yet, right at the present moment, the kind of sterile ventriloquizing of rules Col. Parker succeeded in eliminating in 1873 in Quincy consumes an inordinate portion of time in English classes. It is not uncommon to find, in the face of alarm about student deficiencies in writing, an increase in the amount of time spent in this manner in an attempt to solve the problem. We fail, when we do this, to distinguish between symptoms and causes. How much we *fail to realize.*

We fail to realize that we need not just more old answers to old questions, but, rather, some new questions which will permit new answers and, so, new solutions. It may be that the emergence of a concern for disadvantaged youth can help to further the search for a new English, relevant to our times, by making ways of helping students to learn the focus of attention. It is, alas, quite common to hear English teachers refer to disadvantaged youth in the following terms: "They just don't want to learn." "They just aren't interested." "They just don't have the IQ." "They just don't have the verbal ability." "They don't learn it no matter how many times I teach it."

Notice that the onus is always on the student. *What* is it that they do not want to learn? *What* is it that they are not interested in? How can something be *taught* if no one learns it? Might some of the causes of the problem reside in the fact that much of what passes for "English" is simply irrelevant?

Might it be said that we should be asking how a subject concerned primarily with the role of language and literature in human affairs can best be approached to permit student interest to play a role so that learning, useful learning, can occur? Plato noted that ". . . education can accomplish its goal only if reason has an adequate emotional base."[4] The adequacy of such an emotional base must be judged from student response. To date, such a mode of judgment is rare. The rarity with which such student response is included in determining the *what* and *how* of English is in no small measure a result of the fact that teachers of English are largely uninformed about:

(1) the psychology of learning,
(2) the psychology of communication,
(3) the significance of scientific knowledge about language, and
(4) the significance of cultural changes consequent to technological change.

Such awareness, however acquired, could produce the changes in attitude toward and about the teaching of English that are needed before such teaching can become relevant. One change which might help would be for teachers of English to hold less "moral" attitudes about language. In particular, they might hold a more flexible position reflected in less rigid adherence to unrealistic and unreasonable standards which they, the teachers, characteristically insist upon. Commonly ignored is the fact that students do use language effectively in various ways during virtually every waking moment, and that students are members of a culture. It is merely not the culture of the teacher. Adolescents, and particularly the disadvantaged, may seem to lack verbal ability in the English class because just about every attempt to speak or write is made in the face of the threat of correction commonly made in a manner intended to disparage or ridicule rather than to help.

The most usual kind of attention that student writing, for example, gets from the English teacher is sharply negative: the red pencil is used to slash away at "errors" with a vengeance appropriate to the Old Testament. In this process, we fail to realize that a useful distinction can be made between writing and editing, and that while it is the students' editing ability that is being evaluated (rather than, as is supposed, their writing ability), students have little or no training in editing. The distinction between these two quite different abilities is obscured by what is called composition.

Beyond this is the fact that students seldom have an opportunity to engage in an attempt at real communication by writing about something of significance to themselves for some real purpose to someone whose response they seriously wish to affect. They are doomed to "writing writing," usually, for its own sake, which turns out to mean for a grade. In the face of all this, their lack of writing ability should come as no surprise.

SELF-FULFILLING PREDICTIONS

Much has been said and written about the difference between the middle-class culture of teachers, on the one hand, and the, apparently, nonmiddle-class culture of students, particularly the disadvantaged, on the other. The most critical difference seems to lie in the teachers' perception of and attitude toward these students.[5] To put it simply, the teacher's lot is not a happy one. The English teacher especially seems condemned to chronic frustration as a consequence of adherence to expectations which cannot reasonably be realized. The teacher, as is well known, responds most favorably to students who are neatly dressed, obedient, and who are not noticeably "different." Since most English teachers are women, girls are generally favored over boys. Girls like English much more then boys do. Disadvantaged students, especially boys, most commonly fail to meet these expectations of the teacher, and so they are vulnerable to her disfavor. They are used as "whipping boys," on whom the teacher works out the accumulated frustrations of the job. They have little defense except to drop out of school, and about 1,000,000 a year do just that. Indications are that the English class triggers the drop-out.[6] As Edgar Z. Friedenberg points out, "The most tragic thing that happens to lower-class youngsters in school is that they learn to accept the prevailing judgment of their worth."[7]

INDIVIDUAL DIFFERENCES AND ASSEMBLY-LINE PROCEDURES

With all the talk about individual differences, a careful look at the school as a process quickly reveals that the premium is much more on making students alike than it is on helping them to make the most of their individuality. They are all expected to learn the same thing in the same way at the same time. The pressure is great to make them into standardized, interchangeable parts. The idea of standardized parts permitted a tremendous breakthrough in assembly-line production, but when it is used as a basic metaphor for dealing with human beings it leaves much to be desired. Indeed, as experiments with the ungraded high school suggest, the egg-crate or lock-step arrangement found in most high schools may be one of the major causes of the "problem of disadvantaged youth."

But to illustrate again that the problem is not peculiar to the disadvantaged, and that it may lie more in the structure of the school and the curriculum than in the student, it is worth noting that there are various indications of student discomfort in the face of increasingly dehumanized and mechanized approaches to schooling. The protests of university students about this are increasingly audible. And there is the emergence of the "nego."

It was the boys at Exeter who gave the name "negoism" to the most virulent form of . . . [student] pessimism. This is not crackpot thinking nor is it isolated. It is a fair sample of a deep pessimism prevalent among boys at some of America's finest prep schools. "You don't want to become just a man without a thought—refusing to realize why you are desperate," said a 17 year old at Exeter. "If you face the tough part, and question, and hurt with the questioning, maybe you become someone able to think deeply and clearly. . . . Perhaps my only real doubt is for the survival of sweetness—the survival of warmth and feeling. Is that disallowed nowadays?"[8]

The disadvantaged find Holden Caulfield[9] no less a spokesman for themselves than do the boys at Exeter. They are engaged, just as Holden was, in a search for meaning, and they do not know how to search. We may need something other than a Horn Book approach to "inculcating values." The question is, "What changes in the purposes, functions, and procedures of the school, and particularly in the teaching of English, might be made to help these youth come to grips with their most immediate concerns in ways that permit some resolution?"

AN ECUMENICAL SPIRIT IN EDUCATION

That there needs to be a kind of ecumenical spirit, a willingness to reassess the relevance of English to the world in which we are all attempting to live, generated among those charged with the responsibility for deciding the what and how of it, is coming to be recognized. George H. Henry suggests the need for a "sociology of English." He notes:

Many mathematicians and scientists . . . are perceiving the sociology of their educational task. From Woods Hole, in late 1959, at the Conference on Fundamental Processes in Education sponsored by the National Academy of Science, comes this report: "The processes of education involve, then, four components: a curriculum, the methods of teaching, the context in which the teaching occurs, and, centrally, the teacher." The word "context" here means the forces in the culture that play upon the teaching of mathematics and science—something that few English departments now seriously study or even recognize. What irony that science must remind English departments that English is not an island! In contrast to the scientists, the Modern Language Association has not yet come to this realization.[10]

One cannot help but wonder how it was that our scientific colleagues omitted the learner from their list of ingredients in the processes of instruction. Still, the NAS conference signals an ecumenical spirit in education, even if it is not yet shared by those concerned with the teaching of English.

REASSESSING PURPOSES AND PROCEDURES IN
THE TEACHING OF ENGLISH

This, however, is not to say that pleas have not been made for re-assessing the *raison d'etre* of English. In his presidential address to the National Council of Teachers of English in 1962, G. Robert Carlsen[11] called for a substantive shift away from the teaching of English as facts to be memorized to the active involvement of students in the processes of inquiry. His concern was the student and what happens to the student. It seems clear that Carlsen's remarks were provoked by his awareness of the fact that traditional objectives for the teaching of English were not and are not being achieved. Beyond that, he clearly articulated an aware-ness of the need to include the student in decisions being made about the teaching of English.

One of the most significant attempts ever made to assess ways of teaching literature in high school was in a book by George W. Norvell,[12] while he was supervisor of English for the State of New York. His pur-pose was to identify better means of dealing with literature. It is well worth the time it might take for an English teacher to read. In it, Norvell states:

> It is the well-nigh universal practice in American public schools for a part, at least, of the program in literature to consist of selections studied in common . . . this plan has been vigorously assailed, par-ticularly on the grounds that the reading materials used [selected by teachers and course-of-study makers] were frequently seriously dis-liked by a considerable percentage of the pupils. The result, it was pointed out, was a disgust with the literature rather than a love for it.[13]

> . . . the differences between the interest scores of superior, average, and weak pupils in the same school grades is so small as to be negligible.[14]

Norvell, too, points to the fact that the student must be carefully considered when someone is planning educational activities intended to affect him. It seems that Plato was right all along.

Norvell's report includes a variety of interesting speculations as to what might be done to minimize alienating students while ostensibly teaching them literature. Could it be that the *what* of a subject is insep-arable from the *how* of its being taught? Could it be that all of the strident talk about *content* on the one hand and *methods* on the other obscures the issue by trying to separate the dancer from the dance? In his recom-mendations, for example, Norvell states: "It may well be that . . . the teacher's knowledge of what to *refrain* from recommending is more important than his actual recommendations . . . in view of the high standing both artistically and in children's favor of many modern selections, the use of a large portion of modern literature seems justified."[15]

In the same direction, Frank G. Jennings candidly suggests, "We may have to scuttle some of the shabbily genteel lesson plans we have built . . ."[16] Dora V. Smith and Paul Witty, reviewing studies relating to the effects of the teaching of literature, report, ". . . investigation reveals the need for recognizing the interests of students and attempting to provide a more suitable and varied reading program."[17]

As was previously mentioned, we must note that this problem of the irrelevance of the *content* of English is not peculiar to the disadvantaged. That English has been "out of joint" for some time, and is increasingly so, can hardly be gainsaid.

With the urgings for including modern literature which interests students in a course in English, it should be recognized that the primary literary experience for them, as well as for our society at large, is through television and film, rather than through print. We can ill afford to ignore this fact. Marshall McLuhan,[18] professor of English at St. Michael's College, University of Toronto, refers to the schools as "the first line of defense against media fall-out." It would be naive of English teachers to dismiss too quickly the possibility that he may be right.

For better or for worse (it may depend on whether we attend to McLuhan), the electronic media comprise the essential vicarious experience of adolescents, disadvantaged or not. The Beatles, lest we forget, were recently knighted, much to the dismay of some whose values most closely parallel those of teachers of English.

THE HEART OF THE MATTER

The central problem for all of us is that of developing strategies for survival. This accrues from the central fact of our time: change—massive, rapid, unceasing, accelerating change. As a central strategy, we need to develop ways of assigning viable meanings to the products of the change we constantly confront.

The theater of our time is the "theater of the absurd." Why absurd? What is absurd? It is that to which it is difficult, or impossible, to assign a rational meaning. The theater of the absurd, along with the literature of the absurd, reflects the world of the absurd in which we are all trying, with increasing difficulty, to survive. What could be more absurd than the mosaic of incongruously juxtaposed reports in a daily newspaper? We have difficulty developing a posture from which to view the world about us with some equilibrium, for we lack strategies for assigning meanings to the unceasing swirl of happenings about us. And this problem, too, is by no means confined to the disadvantaged.

A ROLE FOR THE SCHOOL

Edgar Z. Friedenberg suggests a role for the school in dealing with this problem:

> The school exists fundamentally to provide the young people of a community . . . with a fairly tough and firmly fixed philosophical apparatus for making a certain kind of sense out of their lives, and communicating with other people who may be assumed to have basically similar apparatus. . . . [the school's] lack of philosophical structure I should judge to be the chief obstacle to the development of high-school curricula which would use our best cultural resources to help students to make sense out of the lives they actually lead.[19]

What better cultural resources could we use for this purpose than language and literature? Yet, in no quarter of the school "box" is a philosophy (compare with George H. Henry's sociology) for this purpose more lacking than in the teaching of English. In a discipline centrally concerned with the study of language, the philosophy would most appropriately have at its core strategies for assigning meaning, since nothing is more critical to our survival as individuals and as a group than this.

A ROLE FOR ENGLISH

The seeds of such philosophy can be found, perhaps, in the comments above. Indeed, they may already have begun to sprout. In a recent observation, G. Robert Carlsen wrote:

> We all know that a minor revolution has taken place in the teaching of science and mathematics in American schools. Those of us in English suddenly find ourselves faced with a desperate need to catch up. But our attempts to imitate the revolutions in science and math have been based on inadequate understanding of the changes in those fields. While these two areas have changed their content to some extent, they have changed their methodology to a greater extent. The mathematicians and scientists saw clearly that the way a student studies in the subject is fundamental if he is to learn to think within the subject. In English most of our efforts have been in the area of content to be taught. It is time that methods of teaching English again become a major concern within our profession. . . . Methods can usually be described as a choice of one of three roles the teacher selects for himself and his students. . . . Role I: The Teacher Tells—The Student Memorizes and Stores. . . . Role II: The Teacher Molds—The Student Conforms. . . . Role III: The Teacher Stimulates—The Student Teaches Himself. . . . Plato defines the teacher as an "intellectual midwife." . . . My feeling is strong that English at present is

structured to use *telling* and *molding* about 95 percent of the time. We have not really learned as yet how to set up situations in which our students are stimulated and permitted to make discoveries on their own. . . . Inquiry and discovery are the very essence of the reading of literature, yet here too, we as teachers have substituted didacticism and molding.[20]

For reasons that are clear and reasonable, the disadvantaged simply resist this didacticism and molding. The nondisadvantaged merely acquiesce.

Anticipating Carlsen's concern, Arthur W. Foshay reminded us:

Any discipline is a way of knowing—a way of grasping reality. Disciplines differ from one another according to the phenomena they purport to deal with and according to the rules of evidence they employ. By using the rules of a discipline, one may make meaning out of the phenomena it deals with. . . . It is in the making of knowledge that a discipline comes to life, and it is therefore central to the quality of good teaching that the student be drawn into the making of knowledge, according to the nature and rules of the discipline he is trying to learn. In brief, the purpose of studying . . . any discipline is to learn to think the way people in the discipline do. . . . the whole tendency of the pedagogic tradition is toward following the book. We have tried to remove all uncertainty from subject matter. In doing so, we have repeatedly taken the life out of it. In the name of teaching a corpus, we have taught a corpse, and called it a course.[21]

ENGLISH FOR NOW

As was noted at the outset, talking about the problem of disadvantaged youth may be a less fruitful way of getting at needed changes in the teaching of English than talking about the problem of making English relevant. What we have before us is the prospect of restructuring English in a manner which permits the student—disadvantaged or otherwise—to enter with *his* emotional and intellectual experience to participate in inquiries into how language works and what differences it makes, as well as into the literature of the world around him, whether it is in print or some other medium, and in the process discover ways to assign viable meanings to the otherwise meaningless.

It is probably apparent that an attempt is being made here to translate some of the suggestions made by Jerome Bruner into procedures that can be useful in the teaching of English. Neil Postman and Charles Weingartner[22] have described briefly, but with some illustrations, how students can participate and have participated fruitfully in English classes conducted primarily in an inductive manner. The students are not only permitted but encouraged to bring to the inquiry their experience and their meaning as the most essential part of the enterprise. Pursuing inquiries into language, they behave as linguists behave. Inquiring into literature, they behave as literary critics behave. In this latter dimension, the work of I. A. Richards[23] is heavily drawn upon.

This is not studying language and literature for its own sake. As I. A. Richards points out:

> . . . all the questions that matter in literary history and criticism take on a new interest and a wider relevance to human needs. In asking how language works we ask about how thought and feeling and all the other modes of the mind's activity proceed, about how we are to learn to live and how that greatest thing of all, "a command of metaphor" —which is great only because it is a command of life—may best, in spite of Aristotle, "be imparted to another." But to profit we must remember with Hobbes that "the scope of all speculation is the performance of some action or thing to be done," and, with Kant, that "We can by no means require of the pure practical reason to be subordinated to the speculative, and thus to reverse the order, since every interest is at last practical, and even that of the speculative reason is but conditional, and is complete only in its practical use."[24]

It might be said about disadvantaged youth that they agree with Hobbes and Kant. They have no taste for what is not clearly relevant and practical. We might learn something from them.

SUMMARY

In sum, then, what is suggested here is that:

(1) the "problem of disadvantaged youth" may reside more in the what and how of English than in the student;

(2) there are alternatives to placing the onus on the student;

(3) one alternative is to reexamine the reasons given for including English in the curriculum in the first place;

(4) such a reexamination may suggest the need for increasing the relevance of English;

(5) one possible way to do this is to shift from a closed body of content to be covered, to an open inquiry into language and literature through which students can address themselves to cogent questions with some prospect of developing their own answers;

(6) in such a process they can learn how to learn, which is to say that they can learn strategies for assigning viable meanings to the otherwise meaningless.

It is possible to do this. The longer we wait, the longer the disadvantaged, along with everyone else, will be without means of making sense out of their lives.

REFERENCES

1. Quoted in Arthur W. Foshay, "What Is the Message?" *Saturday Review*, February 13, 1960, p. 60.

2. Quoted in Percival M. Symonds, *What Education Has to Learn from Psychology*, Bureau of Publications (Teachers College, Columbia University, 1961), p. 42, from *Francis Wayland Parker: His Life and Educational Reform Work* (New York: E. L. Kellogg and Company, 1900), p. 18.

3. *New York Times*, October 25, 1964, p. E9.

4. The Republic, 536-537.

5. Frank Riessman, *The Culturally Deprived Child* (New York: Harper and Row, 1962), p. 81.

6. Carl L. Byerly, "Pupils Who Do Not Respond," *Educational Leadership*, February 1963, p. 312.

7. Edgar Z. Friedenberg, *The Vanishing Adolescent* (New York: Dell Publishing Co., 1959), p. 117.

8. "The Voice of the Nego," *Life*, Vol. 52, No. 21, May 25, 1962, p. 8.

9. J. D. Salinger, *The Catcher in the Rye* (Boston: Little, Brown and Co., 1951).

10. George H. Henry, "English, the Life of English, and Life," *English Journal*, February 1963, p. 84.

11. G. Robert Carlsen, "The Way of the Spirit and the Way of the Mind," *English Journal*, February 1963.

12. George W. Norvell, *The Reading Interests of Young People* (Boston: D.C. Heath, 1950).

13. George W. Norvell, *ibid.*, p. 83.

14. George W. Norvell, *ibid.*, p. 48.

15. George W. Norvell, *ibid.*, p. 85.

16. Frank G. Jennings, "Literature for Adolescents—Pap or Protein," *English Journal*, December 1956, p. 530.

17. Dora V. Smith and Paul Witty, *NSSE 47th Yearbook*, Part 2 (1948), p. 20.

18. Marshall McLuhan, *The Gutenberg Galaxy* (University of Toronto Press, 1962), and *Understanding Media* (New York: McGraw-Hill, 1964).

19. Edgar Z. Friedenberg, *op. cit.*, p. 75.

20. G. Robert Carlsen, "*How* Do We Teach?" *English Journal*, May 1965, p. 364.

21. Arthur W. Foshay, *op. cit.*, p. 58.

22. Neil Postman and Charles Weingartner, "The New English—A Forward Look," (pamphlet, New York: Holt, Rinehart, and Winston, Inc., 1965).

23. I. A. Richards, *Practical Criticism, Principles of Literary Criticism, Interpretation in Teaching*.

24. I. A. Richards, *The Philosophy of Rhetoric* (New York: Oxford University Press, Galaxy Book, 1965), p. 95.

Focus

One rationale for teacher involvement with extracurricular activities in American high schools was that teachers would get to know the students better and get to see them in contexts other than those apparent in classrooms. As a balance to the Twenties' overpedantic docent, the strategy of teacher involvement was sound, but like so many other sound ideas it was pushed beyond its effective limits when teachers, wearing the hats of cafeteria cop, study hall disciplinarian, bus starter, *et al.*, performed tasks more properly assigned to personnel who were not sacrificing planning and teaching time to logistic rituals.

As originally conceived, too, extracurricular activities assigned to teachers should have extended their academic disciplines. For English, such extensions might be serving as advisers to dramatics, poetry, or film clubs. Extensions of English rubrics in such extracurricular assignments could be explored and reinforced without the onus of a grade inhibiting students' contributions. How teachers permitted themselves to be led into a host of activities unrelated to their training and discipline remains an enigma. But as Mr. Graham points out, there is a crying need to reverse this growing waste of professional talent.

Unlike many writers who lament the unprofessional uses of trained personnel without proposing alternatives, Mr. Graham makes some concrete recommendations for amendments. He then goes on to suggest curricular benefits which might be expected from English teachers released from supervisory rituals, particularly as these curricular revisions apply to so-called school drop-outs.

English Teaching and Drop-outs

ROBERT J. GRAHAM

Grader of Mountainous Composition Piles, Keeper of Hall Discipline, Monitor of Lunchroom Trash, Dispatcher of 6:00 P.M. School Buses, Moonlighting Attendant of Sunday Gasoline Pumps, Frozen Greeter of 7:30 A.M. School Buses—*english teacher*—accept a new title: Scapegoat for the Drop-out!

Protest not, protest not. Worthy thou art, worthy by virtue of a thousand dirty paper cups picked up in a thousand dirty cafeterias.

Sad memories—which comma rules apply here similes Evangeline shows outline and topic sentence Bryant saw these geese meaning death in Greek never forget Leaves 1855–1932–1607 then Silas found Eppie. . . .

Sadder memories—even giving my 144 ninth graders a comp. every other week I have to spend most nights and part of Sunday of course I can handle the cheerleaders along with the yearbook, school newspaper and student council I really am sorry I forgot to inventory the pictures in my room and fill out the forms a play? haven't really had time Updike? Roth? really . . . so little chance to get to but my week on the buses comes after lunchroom duty. . . .

Saddest memories—school . . . what do I want there they don't like me i dont like them beautiful new building? not for me the minute I'm seventeen outta this place what does all that poetry jazz get me why didn't they build one down over the hill for us . . . that ones for college kids Shakespeare—people don't talk like that nowadays over the factory they startcha a hundred a week the minute I'm seventeen. . . .

Scapegoat for the Drop-out, Teacher of Thirty Classes a Week, if you stand on any street corner in any town during the mid-1970's, the cast of your eye, peering through the smog can encompass ten people, probably unemployed, who never finished high school. At that time speaking to some of the 7.5 million drop-outs in the labor force may be the kindest thing you can do. For many who left school, this would be the most personal contact they ever felt with an English teacher. Speaking for them now could obviate the need to speak later.

THE ENGLISH TEACHER

Why the English teacher? Concerned with an area where all meet on common ground, the English teacher has an opportunity and a responsibility that no other professional position can match. English class, the one place students congregate every day from elementary to high school years, takes all knowledge for its realm. Through the frequency with which it meets and the nature of its curriculum, English class can and does exert a lasting impression upon students.[1] That impression can be favorable or unfavorable, inspirational or stagnating, pleasant or painful. Unfortunately, it is all too often the latter of these alternatives for low-ability pupils, those who most frequently become the drop-outs, those most desperately needing language skills.

To many drop-outs the real culprit is not inadequate curriculum, repeated failure, boredom, or frustration; for the seventeen year old doesn't fully understand these things. Usually he sees his nemesis as some vague monolothic monster called "school" or "teacher." Though he may have many specific subject likes, invariably he detests English; furthermore, his hatred often synthesizes into one constant image, the English teacher.[2] In dull class hours he has been plagued by Elizabethan sonnets, vocabulary definitions, and 28 common comma rules. Ironically, he has frequently been thwarted by a teacher who is, himself, thwarted. Overburdened with the school's heaviest academic teaching load, heaviest stack of papers and heaviest extracurricular commitment, the English teacher has all he can do to teach as he has been taught, to run through the same old gambit in the same mechanical way used by so many before him.[3]

Comparing today's high school world with that of 15 years ago is like comparing the Dark Ages with the Age of Enlightenment. However, a vast English teaching army has never had the chance to make that comparison. They have never had the chance because planning time is almost nonexistent, because a week crowded with 25 to 30 classes, plus several onerous duties, plus 75 uncorrected compositions leaves little time to keep abreast of new techniques; indeed, for some it is difficult to avoid intellectual regression.

THE SYSTEM

Compounding the teacher's problem is the "system" he has neither time nor energy to battle. He knows what the potential drop-outs need, but the system is timed to a college future.[4] To make the great gains he has made in the last decade, the college preparatory student has had the help of everyone from mother to school board member. It is just such aid that is denied the noncollege bound. While Ivy bound Bobby is sold on college values, factory bound Billy has little genuine involvement with the working world's values. Yet intense interest and at least partial commitment are exactly the missing factors which would increase his desire to stay in school, at the same time cutting the drop-out rate and strengthening the labor force.[5]

Students with limited ability find it difficult to become involved because they cannot see the relationship between what they study and their personal worlds. Moreover, they are conscious of declining stature just because they are not in the college group and cannot wax enthusiastic over Camus.

Even though only 40 to 60 percent of their graduating classes may be going to college, some secondary school districts build mausoleums whose facilities advertise their status as "college preparatory schools." It is little wonder that students seeing the emphasis placed on language laboratories and planetariums feel such schools are not for them. It is no accident, then, that some schools with highly developed academic elective courses, with special honors and humanities programs—all excellent public relations fodder—totally ignore a high drop-out ratio. The situation becomes more appalling when one learns that only a little more than half the student body is college bound.[6]

Admittedly, the situation will change only when those at the grass roots, teachers in classrooms, exert dynamic leadership. Administrators have been quick to offer statistics, slow to produce program changes. What better person could there be to stimulate change than the English teacher! Certainly it is past time to speak out, to cast off cafeteria and five-a-day bondage; important tasks await.

TWO BASIC ASSUMPTIONS: SOME SPECIFIC SUGGESTIONS

At this point I would like to state some generally accepted assumptions, which are defensible, I believe, on evidence found wherever effective teaching takes place. Implicit within each assumption is the contention that theory must be transformed into practical action.

(1) The atmosphere and attitude facing the noncollege bound student in most schools should and can be adjusted to become a positive rather than a negative force.

Suggestions:

(a) Change *General Curriculum* or other vague and derogatory terms to Career Curriculum.

(b) Provide for the nonacademic pupil's cultural growth just as carefully and appropriately as for the youth headed toward Princeton. Minimum attitudes fostered should encourage desire to read the local newspaper with reasonable discrimination, develop the ability to evaluate cultural and entertainment media, and stimulate concern for the responsibilities of a citizen. If television is to be a major adult entertainment, students should be taught to view it as maturely as possible. Cultural yardsticks are even more valuable for the terminal student than for one who will be influenced by college. A conscious heritage growing from Jack Schaefer's *Shane* is infinitely more desirable than living in an adult world with an undeveloped sense of the American past. Frequently, while a class is scaling the false olympus of *Wuthering Heights*, potential dropouts are planning descent to the army of unemployed.

(c) Offer as much genuine recognition for nonacademic accomplishment as for academic. As well meaning as most teachers and parents are, they certainly have not satisfactorily rewarded nonacademic achievement. When the honor society sponsors an affair, adults turn out willingly; when home economics pupils display sewing skills, it is too often a different story. Certainly some mechanical arts exhibits are as aesthetically meaningful as fine arts displays.

(2) Curriculum change is an immediate need and can be accomplished effectively so that every student finds a measure of success and a reason for being in school.

Suggestions:

(a) Overhaul required reading lists. Although class lists reveal Shakespearean plays and nineteenth century novels in abundance, where are the contemporaries that speak to the nonacademic pupil's situation? Far too few requirements include *Popular Mechanics* along with the *Atlantic*. Boys hoping to spend years fixing carburetors gain more from reading appraisals of 1967 cars than following Silas and Eppie. *Consumer Reports* will provide sentence structures every bit as valid as those in *Harper's*.

(b) Provide close reading and discussion experiences related to students' noncollege bound world. Use John Updike's "A & P," not Henry James' "The Real Thing." Read Phillip Roth's *Goodbye, Columbus and Other Stories* rather than Dickens' *Tale of Two Cities*. Updike and Roth can provide a perceptive look at the occupational world of a nineteen year old and bring to the surface sensitivity many adults think nonexistent. To stimulate these experiences, move desks into small groups; pupils who won't speak out in class will open up in a group of five or six. Help class time come alive.

(c) Devise courses which cross disciplines. Students who detest English but tolerate Commercial Law can get excited about one course covering both, either team-taught or taught by one teacher qualified in both areas. Possible worthwhile combinations are many—limited only by teacher ingenuity and pupil needs—for example, English-Everyday Science, American Studies, English-History of Technology, or English-Contemporary Affairs.

A few years ago John Hersey's practiced eye focused on the educational world with an honesty both comic and horrifying. *The Child Buyer* concerns ". . . a school system informed with rectitude, paper progress, safe activity, hesitation." Here the Chairman, Board of Education, is able to say "Sir, we concern ourselves at Board meetings with bursted boilers. Whether the custodian can be asked to use the gang mower on the football field, that kind of thing. We don't get into educational matters near as much as some people think."

Recently, a Town Curriculum Council, made up of informed citizens, administrators, and teachers (assigned to the committee as a school duty) met in a suburban community allegedly endowed with a fine school system. Using the entire two hours in discussion centered around the cost of school rings, graduation parties, prom gowns, etc., this braintrust adjourned obviously self-satisfied. In the main, subsequent meetings were just as innocuous. Despite an alarming drop-out rate and unbelievably inadequate provisions for low-ability students, this "Curriculum Council" made little mention of curriculum problems during the entire school year. How often is this pattern repeated throughout America?

RECOMMENDATIONS

Unquestionably the time has arrived when school boards and communities must stop hiding drop-out problems, when they must acknowledge and provide for the noncollege bound students. An informed public must recognize this problem for what it is and firmly urge upon its citizens' committees and school officers curriculum adjustments designed to meet the needs as they exist; for the alternative, millions of young people stagnating in a labor force destined to go nowhere because there is nowhere to go, is too debilitating to contemplate.

Superintendents must temper natural urges toward academic temples; they must plan into building additions, as well as new structures, features designed to meet terminal pupils' needs—flexible classroom areas suitable for fused courses, adequate home economic and shop facilities, provision for work experience and service courses.

Teachers, particularly English teachers who reach every student in every school every year, must work hand in hand with citizens. Together they can make school more desirable for those for whom it is terminal education, and in a larger sense update the public school image until it involves all students, getting from all the commitment that makes dead education come alive.

As English teachers become involved in planning effective curricular changes, enthusiasm will become contagious. This kind of involvement will (1) meet the potential drop-out's needs, and (2) modify, then destroy, the scapegoat image. A prerequisite here, however, is vital planning time, recognition that professional time spent on nonprofessional chores is time wasted. Businessmen who used employees with six years of college training to inventory stock or ride herd over lunchrooms would be courting disaster. Though businesslike in many other ways, school administrators think nothing of sending an M.A. in American Literature to load buses, a doctorate in English Education to police cafeteria behavior. Could not inexpensive, part-time lay personnel fulfill such functions? If thousands of hours spent with inane hall, bus, and cafeteria duties ever are converted to creative education, the American school will become what it has rarely been—an exciting place where few can bear to drop out, just because they would miss what is going on.

REFERENCES

1. Hart Leavitt, "To Write or Not to Write: And How?" in Edward J. Gordon (ed.), *Writing and Literature in the Secondary School* (New York: Holt, Rinehart, and Winston, Inc., 1965), p. 56.
2. Carl L. Byerly, "Pupils Who Do Not Respond," *Educational Leadership*, February 1963, p. 312.
3. Edward R. Fagan, "English Methods Courses: Research Perspectives," *Journal of Secondary Education*, April 1964, p. 154.
4. Robert S. Fleming, "Pressure," *The Exchange* (New York: Metropolitan School Study Council, Teachers College, Columbia University), April 1966, p. 11.
5. James W. Guthrie and James A. Kelly, "Compensatory Education—Some Answers for a Skeptic," *Phi Delta Kappan*, October 1965, p. 71.
6. James B. Conant, "Social Dynamite in Our Large Cities," in August Kerber and Barbara Bommarito (eds.), *The Schools and the Urban Crisis* (New York: Holt, Rinehart, and Winston, Inc., 1965), pp. 170–171.

Focus

One of the enigmas faced by those who develop guidelines for educating the disadvantaged is that many of the so-called urban disadvantaged are, in fact, rural disadvantaged. In any metropolis, of course, there are nuclei of second, third, and fourth generation city dwellers, and these urbanites are legitimately the targets of educational programs such as those outlined by Riessman, Deutch, Schreiber, and others. But mixed with these urbanites are recent immigrants to the city whose value systems are essentially rural. Educationally, these rural immigrants might be regarded as first generation urbanites; that is, they are students who live in conflicting cultures. The rural values of their parents are in direct conflict with the urban values of their peers. It is within the confines of this culture conflict that Dallam and Fagan explore the educational guidelines for teaching the urban disadvantaged student and winnow those aspects of the guidelines that seem to have implications for helping the rural disadvantaged student survive in an increasingly technological culture.

These guidelines from study after study imply the need for teacher acceptance of, and adaptation to, change. Change in such a context can be defined as it is in physics, that is, with no strict demarcation of boundaries and with a dynamism that defies prescription. Dallam and Fagan point out that such dynamism makes it improbable that neat content packages for teaching the rural disadvantaged will be available. At the same time, each teacher who works in a rural area has both the potential and the responsibility to use the value systems, the dialects, and the local color of the area in developing viable and kaleidoscopic English programs which, collectively, will give disadvantaged students from rural areas one key to economic survival.

English and Social Survival

EDWARD R. FAGAN
WILLIAM M. DALLAM

Survival, based on English, means many things. To the rural disadvantaged youth it means the ability to score at the fifth-grade level on a test of reading and writing proficiency. If the family farm succumbs to drought, if the coal mine cuts back on personnel, if the clay or brick factory closes down, the rural youth must achieve a fifth-grade literacy level to qualify for the benefits of the Manpower Retraining Act.[1] The impact of the Act's eligibility clause for Pennsylvanians, for example, eliminates almost a million and a half citizens who, according to a 1960 survey, were classified as illiterate (166,000) or as "persons over 25 having less than eight grades of school" (1,400,000). While urbanites might conservatively comprise 70 percent of the figures cited, the 30 percent remaining should be a vital concern for those who hope to educate disadvantaged rural youth.

Survival to the rural disadvantaged youth also means keeping things as they are—keeping kinship bonds and keeping the traditional values and rituals associated with these bonds. Even when, as is often the case, rural families move to the cities to escape the drought, the layoffs in the mines, and the one-industry shutdowns, the rural rituals and values are still cherished as a stable force in an alien environment. In Cincinnati, Ohio, according to Donald Cohen, a sociologist and consultant for the Appalachia Project, one can see on Saturday nights the immigrants to the city attending hoe-downs and indulging in the formal Saturday night patterns of rural Kentucky communities. These rural values are not forgotten by the temporary city dweller either, for the male migrant worker in the city seldom considers the city his home and lives only to make enough money to return to his rural homestead.

Frank Riessman's profile of the urban disadvantaged adult male as described in *The Culturally Deprived Child* is general enough to include the rural disadvantaged, as described by Dallam, and consists of the following:

> He is traditional, superstitious. He reads ineffectively, is poorly in-
> formed in many areas, suspicious of "talk" and "newfangled ideas."
> In some areas he has intense convictions: morality, punishment, cus-
> tom, diet, traditional education—these opinions are not open to reason
> and are not flexible. He feels alienated from society—believes leaders
> are corrupt and hates "big shots." He sees all problems as caused ex-
> ternally, not internally. He is not class conscious. He prefers security.
> He likes excitement; likes to get away from humdrum life. In politics
> it is the candidate he considers, rather than the platform. He is prag-
> matic and anti-intellectual. He seldom uses abstract ideas. He thinks
> through a problem by working on it with his hands. He admires
> strength and endurance. He believes in a man's world—in the Negro
> subculture the mother plays a strong masculine role.[2]

Riessman's profile contains somewhat paradoxical statements, for example, "He prefers security. He likes excitement; likes to get away from humdrum life." Although this is true, the value patterns and their resultant attitudes toward formal education generally reflect a classroom climate for teaching the disadvantaged which every English teacher should consider.

SURVIVAL AND LANGUAGE

Long before the rural disadvantaged youth arrives at the junior high school, he finds himself running on an educational treadmill to oblivion. As early as kindergarten, according to Charles E. Silberman in *Crisis in Black and White*,[3] the disadvantaged child misses about 85 percent of what goes on in a formal classroom. Such children have not been trained to listen. The fact that Silberman is reporting about urban Negroes in the ghettoes does not rule out the fact that the same environment he de-scribes also pertains to the minority groups who comprise the migratory workers of rural communities.

Other deficiencies besides listening, as identified by Martin Deutsch, coordinator of the Institute for Disadvantaged Studies at New York Med-ical College, that have direct bearing on the teaching of English are the following:

> They lack the experience to take tests. The phrase "is to" (as in cat
> "is to" kitten as lion "is to" cub) frequently has no meaning for them.
> Teachers are just now learning to adapt these tests by using the mean-
> ingful expression "goes with."
>
> They don't know how to study. Quite literally these children have no
> place to develop any study skills.

They have "gunshot vision," that is, a very narrow focus of understanding. Much of what the teacher says is not within their experience.
Most of the children, Deutsch says, have not gone farther than two
blocks from home before coming to school.

They lack the experience to generalize while reading. Generalizing
while reading is one of the skills much needed to handle that complex
of abilities called "reading with understanding."[4]

One qualification of Deutsch's generalizations needs to be made for
the rural disadvantaged: instead of students who "have not gone farther
than two blocks from home," the word "hollow" should be substituted
for "home." Hollow, in rural, mountainous areas such as those found in
Appalachia, refers to the geographic boundaries of a speech community.
It is not unusual in talking with rural disadvantaged youth to find that
they have never been over the mountain or into the next hollow; hence
there are provincialisms and locutions which are unique to each hollow
and which need to be understood by English teachers planning strategies
for teaching in a particular hollow.

Where English teachers are to find such information for making an
impact on the rural disadvantaged is a moot question. Federal and private
foundations, through university programs, have made a start in preparing
teachers for work in urban slums, but there are perhaps three universities
in the country which are planning to organize teacher-training programs
for the rural disadvantaged. One indication of the need for new programs
aimed at educating teachers of English in this specialty is implied by
Patricia Sexton's description of general English courses set up for disadvantaged students in rural areas as these programs operate in so-called
comprehensive or joint high schools. Miss Sexton's *Education and Income*
describes the grammar and composition dimensions of general English
courses as follows:

. . . while grammar exercises seem designed to help no one, usage
exercises seemed designed to help only those students (usually from
middle and upper-income groups) who commit minor infractions of
the rules. So it is that continuing references are made in texts to mis-
placed commas, the forms of "lie" and "lay," and the use of "who"
and "whom," dangling participles, etc.

Another complicating problem is that English teachers often have a
sadly limited understanding of what "good" writing looks like, their
view being that it's good if it does not begin with "and" or end with
a preposition. Other than knowing these two rules (which are violated
a thousand times a day by professional writers), they can usually spot
spelling errors and run-on sentences, but much beyond that they
are lost.[5]

Implied by Miss Sexton's description is the failure of universities to provide prospective teachers with principles and concepts for adapting English curricular structures to students' local value systems. In given rural hollow, for example, such an adaptation might begin by finding out just what kinds of English skills are most useful to such students. Or put another way, what English skills do these students need in order to survive? Answers to that question would certainly include:

(1) understanding the impact of organization as a technique in all media, that is, television, films, magazines, newspapers, textbooks, pamphlets, etc.;

(2) criticizing the contents of media according to some system, for example, the Laswell formula, which by its very simplicity might be just the system for the disadvantaged, that is, "Who, says what, to whom, in what media, with what intention?";[6]

(3) involving themselves in experience with language via tapes, records, role playing, dramatic skits, or a class newspaper or magazine;

(4) evaluating all of the foregoing language experiences systematically via constant and immediate feedback which is primarily positive and rewarding.

Overgeneralized though these answers may be, they suggest a few ways for overcoming defects of the sterile general English curriculum described by Miss Sexton. Another means of avoiding deadening "general English" can be found in Ruth Golden's description of Detroit's Changing Dialects Project.[7] As an English teacher in Detroit's inner city schools, Dr. Golden noticed that a frequent reason for rejecting Negro students as salesmen, telephone operators, and the like was that the Negroes could not be "understood." While such reasons may have been rationalizations for discrimination, their frequency prompted Golden to ask, "What English skills do these rejected students need for economic survival?"

To answer that question, Dr. Golden spent a year listening to the speech patterns of Negro students in Detroit's public schools. She noticed the so-called Southern dialect used by Negroes and identified major dialect differences which might be construed as unintelligible by those used to the "standard" midwestern dialect. Based on the findings of her study, Golden developed a series of tapes designed to teach Negro students a second dialect, that of the "accepted" midwestern standard. But the contents of these tapes were based on the assumption that English was a combination of skills—reading, writing, speaking, and listening—so the tapes were designed to improve general English skills, not just speech dialects. The Negroes who participated in Golden's project were not made to feel that their native speech was inferior; instead, they were persuaded that their survival required their ability to shift from one dialect to another as the particular occasion demanded it.

Dr. Golden's procedures might serve as a model for those interested in helping disadvantaged rural youth survive via their English programs. Notice that the Southern dialect identified in her project applied to Appalachian whites as well as to Negroes and that the contents of her program embodied English as a combination of general language skills, as well as specialized skills within those broad areas, for example, vocabulary, spelling, and usage. Notice, especially, that the contents of the English course came from an analysis of the local area, not from some national or regional recommendation. The implication of Golden's focus is that those concerned with developing the English skills of the disadvantaged in rural areas will have to do it hollow-by-hollow.

PRINCIPLES FOR SURVIVAL

Principles for designing survival programs in English for disadvantaged youth in rural areas are implicit in Riessman's conclusions concerning characteristics of the culturally deprived child:

Slowness in performing intellectual tasks is a feature of mental style—a slow child is not necessarily a dull child.

A child may be slow to generalize unless he does something physical with the idea he is trying to grasp.

A deficiency in the use of formal language does not mean a child is nonverbal. Actually, in public language, the deprived child usually is very articulate.

The deprived child responds most directly to audiovisual teaching such as the overhead screen may provide.[8]

Slowness, as Riessman points out, should not be equated with dullness. In some cases deep and complex feelings can be grasped by disadvantaged youth, perhaps because they are disadvantaged. Consider the following sketch of one such student and his poetry as described by Marianne Wolman.

Juan is 17. His father is a cement worker, his mother a nurses' aide. He is a very shy, sensitive boy who has many fears. His mother is greatly concerned about him and gets in touch with Juan's teachers and counselor often. He has an expressive face and looks and acts much more alert than his 82 I.Q. would indicate. Because of his great fears individual testing was suggested. He scored 105 on the Wechsler with a considerably higher score on the performance than on the verbal test. The English Co-operative Test placed him on the 0 percentile. His achievement in all his school subjects is very low.

Wind
There is a wind, I hate to hear,
A wind of mystery and fear.
They say when it is near,
Its voice will call,
"Come here," "come here."
There is a wind, I hate to hear,
A wind of death, a wind of fear.
It's coming! It's voice is near.
Listen, listen, can't you hear?[9]

Based on Juan's English Co-operative Test score and his group I.Q. score, many English teachers would say that poetry would be an impossible focus for Juan. Yet with an understanding teacher and her encouragement, Juan has crystallized a feeling that must haunt many disadvantaged students.

Within Riessman's other three points are the principles of discovery, success, and multisensory stimuli—all basic for teaching the disadvantaged. Detailed applications of these principles will be found later in this book, but, for now, their generalized implication is that concrete objects, reinforced by many media, should be used in a system based on variety (a shift to different topics every fifteen or twenty minutes) which will give students the opportunity to be successful in their learning of the topics presented.

Charles Savitzky, coordinator of the STEP program in New York City, recommended principles similar to those given by Riessman when he pointed out at a Philadelphia curriculum meeting that:

The deprived child is greatly encouraged by many small successes along the way—one of the features of programmed learning.
He is most secure, when handling language problems, in informal situations.
He is most interested in literature that emphasizes human rights and human relations.[10]

Savitzky's principles, like Riessman's, evolved from his work with the urban disadvantaged but apply equally well to the rural disadvantaged. Materials for applying Savitzky's third principle are available for urban students but need to be developed for disadvantaged students in rural areas. Hopefully, ingenious teachers would use some of these urban models and adapt them to rural students' interests.

CONCLUSIONS

Survival for disadvantaged youth from rural areas depends to a large extent on the effectiveness of these students' English program. Classroom behavioral differences between urban and rural disadvantaged students, though few, are significant. Disadvantaged urban youth are more liable to be hostile and aggressive toward education, whereas disadvantaged rural youth are liable to be apathetic or withdrawn within the formal school situation. Both groups look upon education as a useless, adult controlled screening device which spindles them on a skewer marked *failure*.

Changing such value systems at the junior high school level is difficult, and, realistically, the percentage of success for such change is low. But the application of the truisms and principles previously described by Riessman, Savitzky, and others increases the probability for teacher success. That the classroom teacher must be the source for changes in English programs for disadvantaged youth in rural areas is clear. By the teacher's use of the foregoing principles as a base for selection and application of new materials, the disadvantaged youth in rural areas should discover that there are concepts in English which can help him to survive in an increasingly complex world.

But the magnitude of the English teacher's search, adaptation, and application of interesting materials goes beyond the merely practical, which, according to Silberman, is exemplified by James B. Conant's recommendation for more technical high schools. In criticizing Conant's recommendation, Silberman points out that survival for disadvantaged youth must be based on the fact that "The task [of the school today] is to turn out people educated beyond the level previous societies demanded only of their ruling elite."[11] Silberman's charge to the English teacher is to eschew the mundane, the here and now, and to focus on those aspects of contemporary society that require intelligent choices by the students in rural disadvantaged areas. Upon these intelligent choices—political candidates, job selection, vocational aspirations, critical evaluation of mass media, self-identification—rests students' survival in disadvantaged rural areas.

REFERENCES

1. Quoted in William M. Dallam, "English in Relation to Social Needs," *Journal of General Education*, 17, 45-54, April 1965, p. 50.

2. William M. Dallam, *ibid.*, p. 46.

3. Charles E. Silberman, *Crisis in Black and White* (New York: Random House, 1964).

4. William M. Dallam, *op. cit.*, p. 47.

5. William M. Dallam, *op. cit.*, p. 49.

6. Harold D. Laswell, "The Structure and Function of Communication in Society," in Lyman Bryson (ed.), *The Communication of Ideas* (New York: Harper & Brothers, 1948), p. 37.

7. Ruth Golden, "Slow Learners—Instructional Tapes and Insight," *English Journal*, **51**, 418-421, September 1962, p. 420.

8. William M. Dallam, *op. cit.*, p. 52.

9. Marianne Wolman, "Cultural Factors in Creativity," *Journal of Secondary Education*, **37**, 454-460, December 1962.

10. William M. Dallam, *op. cit.*, p. 53.

11. Charles E. Silberman, *op. cit.*, p. 253.

Focus

Heuristics, discovery as process, is not often used in classrooms of disadvantaged youth because the stereotype of the disadvantaged is a student who has a short attention span, must be kept in his place, and must deal with highly concrete material. Popularized by Jerome Bruner (*Process in Education*), heuristics is more and more becoming a technique for newer programs in all disciplines because it comes closest to that definition of learning which maintains that not only must increased academic awareness be the outcome of a learning experience but also *observable behavior change*. Marshall McLuhan (*The Gutenberg Galaxy, Understanding Media*) has long pioneered heuristics as a classroom strategy for learning, and early in 1966, McGraw-Hill released a film, "Child of the Future," which demonstrates McLuhan's thesis about what happens in classrooms where heuristics (or inductive teaching) is the pivotal learning strategy. What is remarkable about the film is that the observed learning is as apparent among preschool children as it is among Ph.D. candidates who represent the range of learning levels presented within the film. Most important, the film gives concrete illustrations of the learnings which occur in classrooms comprised of slow learners and disadvantaged students.

Common to heuristics and to Mr. Graham's discussion of an "open" class is the truism that teachers do not teach; instead, students learn. We might add that they learn only that which they want to learn, material which they define as interesting and useful. Teacher responsibility in a student learning situation is to model and then guide the learning behavior. Students who have never had responsibility for structuring their learning need some guidance, particularly the disadvantaged students who are suspicious of the whole enterprise. But that such students, after overcoming initial suspicions, will eagerly take initiative and responsibility for learning is amply illustrated, with guidelines for structuring such learning, in the article which follows.

English and the Polylogue

ROBERT J. GRAHAM

Disadvantaged youth have a way of growing into disadvantaged adults. How else did the world's most affluent nation acquire

> ... some 3,000,000 shacks, hotels, tenements. . . .[1]
> ... population densities up to 100 people per acre. . . .[2]
> ... migrant workers still earning fifty cents an hour despite minimum wage and poverty guidelines. . . .
> ... miles of billboards flaunting chlorphyl-painted oaks where shortly before the real thing stood. . . .
> . . . adult picture-books selling in the millions while the *Herald-Tribune* dies, and the *New Republic* is read by only a fraction of the number palpitating after *Playboy*. . . .
> ... 40 to 50 million people who ". . . have inadequate housing, medicine, food, and opportunity."[3]

Maybe we are all disadvantaged, but those who get the official title, I sometimes feel, do so because we educate them for it.

Decade after decade, automatic teacher responses to those resisting learning—either through apathy or aggression—have too often included fortified controls, increased teacher-centered materials and activities, and minimal student involvement. Despite all this, everyone *does* learn, perhaps more *out of* than *in* school, certainly more in agreeable situations than in trying ones. In plain truth, teacher-dominated classrooms rarely encourage student-involved experiences. If learning is an *active* process, then the more actively involved the student, the more meaningful should be the gain in knowledge.

PREMISE: SELF-DIRECTION

How pleasant it is to work at something enjoyable; how difficult to concentrate on tiresome chores. Though time goes swiftly by when we are involved, moment drags upon moment if we are not committed to our endeavors. Often it seems impossible to get down to work or to maintain interest once we do; on other occasions, some driving concern propels us onward. So it is for teacher *and* for pupil, in *and* out of school, because, quite appropriately, coupled with involvement, a willing receptiveness does make a difference that counts. Yet, bound by tradition, our teaching of the unwilling learner has until recently moved in a direction antithetical to this basic premise.

Further, there exists a compelling social argument for pupil self-direction in learning situations. Analyzing "Open v. Closed Classrooms," Mario D. Fantini has said:

> We hear a great deal these days about the open v. the closed society. In the one camp we have the totalitarian social order, referred to as a "closed" society, wherein individuals are actually subservient to the state. In the other camp we have those societies which value the individual over the state and are referred to as "open" societies. It is said further that in one society the individual is "free"; in the other, that he is not.
>
> . . . there is a parallel between societies and the classrooms in which teachers find themselves. There are also open and closed classrooms, which, in a sense, are miniatures of open and closed societies.[4]

PREMISE: OPEN CLASS

In an era when the awesome weight of democratic process, mass culture, and economic complexity presses ever more heavily upon the uneducated, the schools' obligation to educate for an open society is incontestable. However, traditional focus fails to prepare students to accept the individual responsibilities soon to be forced upon them. For pupils—especially unwilling learners—academic freedom and cooperative planning are nearly nonexistent in the classroom, even though scant months after leaving school, by whatever route, youngsters must bruit the world of individual decision, must act and react upon a value base, must employ rational skills, and must stifle or nurture aspiration. Ironically, those students who most need training for an open society are blocked from it. Unprepared, they are pushed into militant unionism or tacit withdrawal. Little more than polarities between active and passive nonentity, either choice is a defense against a world they have not made.

THE PROBLEM

Untrained to think for themselves, accustomed to accepting others' standards, disadvantaged adults find it as easy to adopt group beliefs as it was to agree with the dominant crowd in school, as painless to support inept politicians as it was to let teachers pull acceptable answers from uncritical minds. To guarantee thought-free leisure, they need only tune their television to whatever advertisers say is the year's best. After all, "The Beverly Hillbillies" is understandable; it's not couched in panting pentameters or set in Brobdingnag—at least not in Swift's Brobdingnag!

Do the boys now sitting in the classrooms of the sixties, those who will grow into the men sketched above, have a chance? Will they ever know a better way than they now have for distinguishing illusion from reality? How much lifetime can they squander on generalization and half-understood truths, on superficial brushes with beauty, and on a pseudo-identity assumed because they never found out what fulfilled potential might have brought?

INTERPERSONAL DESIGN FOCUS

Building upon the implications of an open society system translated into an open classroom approach, teachers can, I feel, utilize designs which provide opportunities for growth in student perception. To me, the most effective patterns can be structured around *interpersonal designs*. By this term I mean a planned linking of content and technique to produce opportunities for positive interaction which encourages self-understanding as well as growth in attitude, behavior, and insight. Less observation— especially of teacher-models—and more interaction with peers, community-models, and the culturally different are the keys. Materials for such teaching are everywhere; they need only be recognized and meaningfully implemented. Old materials must be used in new ways; fresh materials can and must be devised to both nurture and illustrate new modes of thinking about ancient problems.

Though all divisions are arbitrary, and there is desirable overlapping, I suggest three design categories.

(1) Informational: Accurate cognitive learning is necessary since there is no understanding without knowledge and one must learn to differentiate between what is and what is not.

(2) Instrumental: Though knowledge assaults illusion, tools adaptable to changing situations (somewhat like adjustable wrenches) are needed.

(3) Confrontational: Remembering Jerome Bruner's dicta concerning man's resistance to surprise and "brutal selectivity" of perceptions, one must force this surprise, provide disorientating experience, undress stereotypes, and reclothe individuals.

Since the first category is obvious—discriminating choices in bibliography, film, and mass media are imperative here*—let's examine an

---

* There is a pressing need to include materials on the culturally different; for example, most English programs are woefully weak in Latin American, Asiatic, and other nonwestern world literature.

interpersonal design covering the latter two, a modified version of S. I. Hayakawa's "Abstraction Ladder."[5] Simple and direct, an effective design might proceed as follows:

(1) Arrange chairs in groups of five or six prior to students' arrival.

(2) As class begins, flash an abbreviated ladder, made into a colored transparency for overhead projector use, onto a wall or screen.[6]

5. wealth
4. farm asset
3. Bessie
2. cow^2
1. cow^1

(3) Briefly explain the functions inherent in levels illustrated on the ladder, emphasizing what is omitted as one reads up the ladder.

(4) After it is apparent that pupils understand the ladder, ask each group to:

    (a) select a spokesman;

    (b) construct its own ladder utilizing a brand name automobile;

    (c) be prepared to explain and defend its choices.

One group effort produced the following:

5. cool reputation
4. lots of money
3. hot car
2. Mustang
1. Ford

(5) When it seems appropriate, request each spokesman to display his group's ladder; encourage the entire group to answer questions about its selections. Stay out of the way unless needed!

(6) The next meeting—with students in different groups—mention that you have a real challenge for them: build a ladder using Negro, Jew, Puerto Rican, Greek, or Russian on level one. Follow the same procedures as above.

The stage is now set for the part that counts most, transference from labels and stereotyped terms to faulty concepts and unsupportable generalizations. But even before the teacher sparks pupils to begin ladders with "Puerto Ricans are sneaky" or "Negroes are lazy" or "Russians are dangerous" it will be apparent that students are involved, are committed.

This commitment is sincerely made because English class no longer seems "out of it," a place where they bother you with things never used, but rather a place to study about life, about things "important to me." Through group dynamics and increased student responsibility, the English classroom takes on a contemporary importance, a meaningful immediacy, almost a life context.

DESIGN INSTRUMENTS

Armed with such instruments as the abstraction ladder, adaptable tools which can be used in varied situations, students have little difficulty recognizing the problem of relating words to things.* Soon they realize that the word is not the thing and that definitions ignore differences between yesterday and today. Pyramiding this new learning, the teacher can stimulate application of the ladder to newspaper and magazine reading. It takes remarkably little practice for general curriculum students to consistently spot speakers or writers who operate at high abstraction levels. That far too many people react to the abstraction rather than to the individual person or idea can soon be understood by all. Further, to encourage confrontation with the epithets of the twentieth century is to structure opportunities for learners to bring about their own growth through self-evaluation of attitudes and values.

A UNIT DESIGN

Among the disadvantaged, none are more maligned than the sizable number many schools relegate to the "general" curriculum. "Man as a Seeker," a year's theme in General English, sophomore level, was one high school's answer to Professor Fantini's lucid comments on open versus closed classrooms. Following thematic approaches based on selected paperbacks and library references, this class studied man through close analysis of his creative and vocational expressions, that is, his work, literature, art, architecture, and music. A four marking period school year suggested the following organization: man searching (1) for himself; (2) for a place in society; (3) for a national identity; (4) for the ideal.

Since these sophomores had not previously experienced open classroom methods, early meetings were devoted to orientation. Informally, students were asked what they would consider worthwhile activity areas for a sophomore class, what they felt their urgent language needs, what endeavors would best prepare them for the responsible freedoms of adult

---

* Hayakawa's concepts of two-valued orientation, purr-snarl word usage plus teacher-student developed value guidelines for television viewing and magazine and newspaper reading are excellent instrument possibilities.

life. Gradually, though unbelievingly, pupils realized they could help plan class activities, regulate reading and writing assignments, participate in self-evaluation sessions, prepare long-range classroom schedules, and discipline themselves to work with minimal supervision. Except for scheduling and activities, a large portion of the first unit's requirements were planned by the teacher. Each succeeding unit would find class members assuming increased responsibility. Finally, the last unit, a search for the ideal, would be predominantly student-planned with the profound hope that the learner himself would become the seeker.

PROCEDURES

Explaining that each student would be responsible for depth work in one specific project, the teacher announced a common reading list and the project areas for Unit 1.

Area	Reading
(1) the self and others	dittoed poetry booklet: Cummings, "Poem, or Beauty Hurts Mr. Vinal"; Auden, "The Unknown Citizen"; Robinson, "Richard Cory"
	John Updike, "A & P"; also contemporary magazine articles
(2) the self and war	Crane, *The Red Badge of Courage*
(3) the outdoors as source of good and evil	Hemingway, *The Old Man and the Sea*
(4) the "outsiders"	Salinger, *Nine Stories*
(5) the self in nonprint media	library-reference group

Divided into five groups, each with a primary duty to learn about one basic area, students held their first meetings. Enthusiastic hands reached for crisp, new paperbacks. Vague yearnings sent some pupils to Hemingway's fisherman, others to the chaos of civil war, still others to the Glass family's chimerical world. One group was assigned periodical readings on the theme plus library reference responsibility, that is, research into general aspects not covered by those working in specific areas. In succeeding units, groups would be shuffled, each pupil serving with the reference committee once during the year. At first, pertinent suggestions were offered this group, but basically it was expected to search out a worthwhile tangent of the unit theme unexplored by an assigned team.

The major group obligation was to its classmates, for a comprehensive understanding of a particular work rested upon each committee's ability to present its material accurately and interestingly. Bull session, panel, debate—whatever the approach—each group accepted the challenge to perfect meaningful and creative classroom activity.

SCHEDULE

Four weeks later, a typical class or student committee-planned schedule revealed:

Monday—GIL (group, individual, or library) time;

Tuesday—round-table discussion, "Kinds of Courage: Where *I* Stand," led by library-reference group;

Wednesday—continue round-table discussion;

Thursday—GIL;

Friday—GIL, meetings of: self-evaluation committee, schedule planning committee;

Monday—group progress reports;

Tuesday—*John Brown's Body*, Benet, taped performance;

Wednesday—continue *John Brown's Body*; discussion: "Where does loyalty end and betrayal begin?";

Thursday—conclude discussion; timed writings (at home) on theme-related topic;

Friday—GIL.

Scheduled GIL time means that a student may plan to meet with a project group, work independently, or pursue library research. One such day found:

(1) two boys from library-reference team taping readings from a recording of "In White America" interspersed with correlated or background music chosen from folk songs, spirituals, and rock and roll ballads;

(2) members of the "self and others" group downstairs in a recreation room previewing the powerful CBS documentary, "16 in Webster Groves" prior to assessing its value for the whole class;

(3) pupils using a vacant classroom to rehearse a dialogue between Sammy, the teen-ager in Updike's "A & P" and Mr. Vinal, the soured inconoclast in Cummings' poem—they had cooperatively written the dialogue;

(4) teacher holding group or pupil conferences;

(5) students reading in class or doing reference work in school or nearby community library.

It must be emphasized that these were student-initiated activities. Rare, indeed, are day-to-day assignments. Work designated for the nine-week period must be accomplished through self-discipline, through group dynamics, group members working interdependently toward a primary responsibility: presentation of newly gained knowledge and understanding to the entire class.

A word to the skeptic: though every teacher has experienced surprise at what pupils accomplish when they know we are counting on them, too few teachers utilize this lever with reluctant learners. An increasing body of responsible research, such as the Banneker Project in St. Louis, Missouri, indicates a strong correlation between achievement and expectation.[7] As Kenneth B. Clark succinctly puts it:

> "Culturally deprived" children have learned in those public schools in which they are expected to learn and in which they are taught.[8]
>
> . . . deprivation is less important in their success than other factors— such as the faith of the teachers, the quality of the education. The common denominator in all these successful programs was more efficient teaching—these children can be taught if they are accepted and respected.[9]

OBSERVATIONS

(1) *After a number of years of experimentation, I am firmly convinced that this method exhibits decisive superiority over closed instruction, especially in English and history classrooms.* Students become involved; students become committed. Products of lecture-recite-test methodology, they have been rewarded for conformity, for unimaginative leadership. In an idea-centered classroom, where nonconformity is used to encourage creativity, pupils have greater incentive to explore. There is time—individual time—to foster love of learning, to reflect upon thoughts culled from reading, and to expand such thoughts into logical concepts.

Within the unit framework, the schedule remains flexible enough to meet urgent needs. Thus, the teacher can capitalize on pupil enthusiasms without the pressure to finish *Silas Marner*, Part II and without inane anthologized limitations. Recently, GIL rescheduling permitted a class to follow one of its member's suggestion that it view the movie version of *West Side Story*. This recommendation resulted in a valuable class experience, threw further light on the theme, and culminated in movie reviews written by the students.

(2) *The class must be pupil-directed as well as idea-centered.* Commenting on the teacher's role in the open system, Professor Fantini mentions the teacher as a "climate setter." Not only must the teacher provide the proper atmosphere, he must do it as unobtrusively as possible. In short, *he must know how to stay out of the way.* He must resist the temptation to tell. Often, suggestions must be vague—so subtle that they are no more than a spark set to the roman candle of a student's mind. Fireworks will begin! Have no fear! But when the spark ignites, the teacher must fade into the background, letting creativity blaze its course. When a group becomes hopelessly entangled, they will ask for advice. Even then the teacher must not allow the pupilcentric structure to be replaced by a teachercentric one.

(3) *The teacher must be an innovator who is sold on the open method.* Coupling natural enthusiasm and worthwhile activity, the teacher can anticipate lagging spirits and frustrated efforts. From time to time all classroom work, group projects included, must be stimulated. A new book passed to students with genuine relish often works wonders. A film catalogue handed to pupils with the offhand comment that "something in here might work well with your presentation" can set young minds working at a feverish pace. Fresh, mind-catching materials are all about us and need only to be recognized by student and teacher alike. However, the best stimulant remains wholehearted, excited interest in student progress. Fortunately, enthusiasm is contagious, and some teachers seem constantly infected.

(4) *The teacher must exude confidence in students' ability to work independently and maturely.* So little that we do on the secondary level prepares pupils for the freedoms they will have in an open society! In June, English teachers are busy checking daily assignments for youngsters who, three months later, may be expected to work alone or with limited supervision. An open class allows pupils to develop self-direction, to find their own methods of getting things done. Moreover, sincere respect for creativity, for ideas, and for intellectual leadership grows along the way. Somehow, those concepts foisted upon us or just handed down as land-grants are never as meaningful as those we stumble upon ourselves. Students soon learn that wasted GIL time has been expensively purchased. Before long, they are aware of the folly evident in nonexistent or haphazard planning.

(5) *Open classrooms foster interdependence between disciplines.* Subject fusion is a natural by-product of thematic group work, for the teacher focuses upon evolving trends and developing broad concepts, always striving, as he proceeds, to enable students to see the complete panorama. Thus, interdisciplinary parallels are encouraged. Comparisons between the means used by a journalist and a poet in depicting an auto

wreck, between democracy and Emersonian individualism, between chauvinism in a patriotic blurb and in a nation's architecture are eagerly sought and thoughtfully interrelated. Now, students are not so prone to label one class pure literature, the next straight history. The symbolism of art, religion, Gallup polls, folk songs, discount houses, magazines, and social problems is a significant part of the experience matrix. Knowledge is best spawned in a life context, for, as Professor Fantini points out, the open classroom ". . . is a replica of the open society."[10]

REFERENCES

1. Michael Harrington, *The Other America* (Baltimore, Maryland: Penguin Books, 1964), p. 137.
2. Kenneth B. Clark, *Dark Ghetto* (New York: Harper and Row, 1965), p. 30.
3. Michael Harrington, *op. cit.*, p. 54.
4. Mario D. Fantini, "Open v. Closed Classrooms," *The Clearing House,* **37**, 67-71, October 1962.
5. S. I. Hayakawa, *Language in Thought and Action* (New York: Harcourt, Brace, and World, 1964). Chapters 10, 11, and 12 treat problems of naming, defining, and abstracting.
6. S. I. Hayakawa, *ibid.*, p. 179. Though Hayakawa's ladder utilizes eight levels, the five used here seem understandable and interesting to disadvantaged learners.
7. Kenneth B. Clark, *op. cit.*, pp. 143-144; or see Chapter 6 in its entirety.
8. Kenneth B. Clark, *op. cit.*, p. 141.
9. Kenneth B. Clark, *op. cit.*, p. 146.
10. Mario D. Fantini, *op. cit.*, p. 69.

Focus

Using principles from both psychology and sociology, educational psychologists specialize in the etiology of the teacher-learning process. In their search for causes they continually relate parts to wholes and thereby set up an interdisciplinary field where dynamism is basic and boundaries are constantly shifting. Attempting to make generalizations about the educational process under such dynamic circumstances is something like examining six inches of an eighteen-foot boa constrictor clamped into a vise—and just about as dangerous.

Educational psychologists, despite their tenuous ability to control variables, sometimes discover testable generalizations; at other times, they provide useful tools for the classroom teacher to assess students' learning behavior. In the area of generalizations, Herbert A. Thelen in a paper given at the Pennsylvania State University made a useful distinction between "engagement" and "learning." He leads up to the distinction when he writes:

> Schooling is expected to alter their [students] behavior through (a) causing them to *engage in* certain activities (e.g., reading, experimenting) they are not likely otherwise to engage in, and (b) supervising this participation in such a way that the child will *learn* from it the lessons we think are important. Engagement and learning are two different things . . . for example, it is possible for a child to go through a programmed text, making all the required responses correctly, and not remember any of the ideas he has been dealing with. . . . It is possible for a child to study spelling for seven years and not be able to spell.*

What children learn in such a context, Thelen maintains, is socialized role playing. Later he documents this judgment by citing a general factor exhibited by 750 students from Chicago schools, grades 7 through 11, as "submissiveness, dependency on the teacher, and an undiscriminating

---

* Herbert A. Thelen, "Some Classroom Quiddities for People-Oriented Teachers." Department of Educational Psychology, University of Chicago, April 1965, p. 1 (mimeographed).

liking for all classroom activities."* What these students lack, Thelen states, is involvement, commitment to the point where behavior change occurs—doing something to show that they have learned, for example, taking part in "issues" such as civil rights.

Concerning the disadvantaged, Thelen implies that curricular guides, based on socially acceptable educational roles, teach students little but role playing. It is, ultimately, teacher interaction and evaluation of curricula and students that determine whether learning has occurred. Mr. Withall's Index was designed with that specific purpose in mind. Confined to verbal behavior, the Index nevertheless serves as a beginning effort to assess with validity and reliability the climates favorable to student learning as defined by educational psychologists.

* Herbert A. Thelen, *ibid.*, p. 4

Learning and Classroom Climate

JOHN WITHALL

One of the major disadvantages that overtakes human beings who are raised in an impoverished area is their lack of communication skills; hence the need for Project Head Start.* The day-to-day cares of disadvantaged adults in getting and using the limited food, clothing, and other essentials demand too much time, energy, and attention to permit them to talk with their children. Since such adults have limited time to talk with, to socialize, or to play with their children, the children get little or no exposure to daily speech as the medium for social interaction.

Another handicap suffered by the culturally disadvantaged is their lack of books, pictures, magazines, and newspapers which are a major source of knowledge for middle-class children. The printed page is rarely encountered by youngsters from disadvantaged backgrounds; yet print is the mainstay of schools, teachers, and the educational process in our culture. Learners who have had little or no contact with these media in their early years are at a disadvantage as soon as they enter learning situations which depend on oral and written language.

This disadvantage in the classroom is compounded by the fact that the teachers who are trying to help learners to learn frequently take for granted a middle-class value system which is unknown or at best unfamiliar to their charges. Middle-class values such as thrift and parsimony in use of material objects are foreign to disadvantaged students. Inhibition of fighting, practice of social amenities, aggression through words rather than acts, and an ability to forego immediate for later rewards are other middle-class values which teachers try to impose on confused disadvantaged children.

---

* Project Head Start is a national effort to expose disadvantaged youngsters to the stimulation of an educational experience under the guidance of trained adults who will help the youngsters to experience, practice, and enjoy the communication skills they tend to lack.

It must be a strange and uneasy feeling for young learners to move into a situation where spoken and written communication, an unfamiliar value system, and subtly defined behavioral limits are imposed. Small wonder they are unable to master effectively the school-imposed information and skills. If they see some of their more advantaged peers achieving with ease, this must disturb them even more. Teachers have to use strategies and adopt teaching procedures to help disadvantaged learners to be more at home with the unfamiliar. These students need help in understanding the totally *foreign* cultural setting* and in exploring, with a sense of security, the data and skills being offered to them. As Brain has said, "One quality a teacher of the disadvantaged should possess can be characterized as a personal warmth. The teacher may express warmth in many ways, by physical contact, by listening when children talk, by the kind of understanding typified by a parent. . . ."[1]

LEARNING CLIMATES

There is some evidence in research literature[2] that a learning climate can be created which will help to reduce the threat that learning situations often involve. Such a climate helps learners to organize their mental and emotional resources more fully to deal with the learning problem. This liberating climate occurs when teachers use the following procedures:

(1) verbalize to the learners encouragement and commendation for effort and achievement that merit such praise;

(2) indicate a readiness to entertain and seriously consider an idea, suggestion, or explanation that is offered by the learners;

(3) hear out when learners make a contribution and communicating to the learners that the message was received and comprehended;

(4) raise problem-oriented questions and make problem-oriented statements to assist the learners to focus on the task:

(5) encourage goal identification and definition by the learners.

Talk about helping the disadvantaged, about affording them educational and cultural advantages, is useless unless the message gets to them. It is not the meaning they get from such talk but the meaning they give to such talk that helps them to know concepts, ideas, values, insights, and knowledge. Unless these learners are psychologically freed to discover and to think about ideas and concepts, and to give meaning to these sources of wisdom, no amount of exposure to audio-visual aids, to field

* Some of the elements of overseas cultural shock—disorientation, inability to focus on surroundings, psychological trauma, and resulting random withdrawing or attacking behaviors—like that experienced by sensitive travellers abroad overtake disadvantaged youngsters in school.

trips, or to enrichment activities will help. Disadvantaged students have to be released—we might even say unleashed—psychologically and emotionally in order to decode the school's and the teachers' messages.

In the classroom the teacher must be concerned with both the *socio* and *psyche* needs of the learner.[3] The socio needs, simply stated, are the needs to carry out or to participate in completing a task or in resolving a problem. The task may be playing in a band, contributing to a class discussion, building a mock-up of the latest space module, solving an equation, or participating in choral speaking. Such activities are not exclusively but are primarily socio-need oriented. The psyche needs of learners are the recognized needs of human beings for being with and interacting with compatible individuals (usually peers) whom they like and who like them. Most recreational and play groups (for example, bridge clubs, golf foursomes, tennis partners, and picnic groups) based on friendship and family affinities are of this sort. If the socio tasks or achievement learning tasks in the classroom are to be successfully accomplished, the teacher must deliberately seek to appreciate and to attend to the learners' psyche needs. How can this best be done?

LANGUAGE AND LEARNING CLIMATES

The work of Flanders,[4] Perkins,[5] Polansky,[6] and Withall[7] indicates that the social-emotional classroom atmosphere created by the teacher's verbal and nonverbal behaviors has a demonstrable influence on the problem solving and learning activities of learners.[8]

With the use of an instrument entitled the Social-Emotional Climate Index, it is possible to describe and categorize classroom climates or group problem solving situations. The instrument involves the categorization of the verbal behaviors of the teacher or leader into one of seven categories.* Depending on whether the verbalizations fall in larger proportion into the first three categories (learner-oriented)—praising, accepting-clarifying, and problem solving categories—or the last three categories (teacher-oriented)—directing, reproving, and teacher supportive categories—the resultant climate may be dubbed either learner-centered or teacher-centered. The fact that the Index allows teachers to discover their classroom climates and to plan more learner-centered strategies for their disadvantaged students does not mean that this discovery will put the disadvantaged students so much at ease psychologically that their blocks to learning will be removed. Rather, teachers' increased awareness via the Index should enhance their understanding and sensitivity to learners and thereby reduce somewhat the insecurity and sense of inadequacy that is too often apparent in disadvantaged classrooms.

* See criteria for the seven categories in Appendix B.

Since disadvantaged students carry with them their own special brand of free-floating anxiety, and since they are foreigners in their middle-class school situation, they need a learning atmosphere which gives them the security necessary to help them attack the socio problems in the classroom within a psychological situation that satisfies their psyche needs. The teacher's behavior, verbal and otherwise, in this situation determines the extent to which such an enhancing learning climate is realized. If the teacher demonstrates an understanding of the disadvantaged learner's plight, he can help to determine the kinds of relationships between learner and teacher and between learner and learner that occur in the classroom. With that information he can then influence the quality and quantity of student achievement.

That a liberating learning climate is a boon to all learners goes without saying, but for the socially and culturally disadvantaged it is the *sine qua non* of effective classroom effort. Operationally, climate may be defined or measured in terms of the proportion of the teacher's verbalizations that fall into the learner-centered as opposed to teacher-centered categories of the Index. Climate can be described, too, as the resultant of the teacher's genuineness in his behaviors towards the learners. This genuineness emerges from the clear readiness of the teacher to accept the learner as he is, a readiness to allow himself to be used as a learning resource, and a readiness to view the learning problem and situation from the frame of reference of the learners.[9]

The essence of this paper is that if this liberating learning climate is created by the teacher for disadvantaged students, then they can be helped to see the people and world about them with different frames of reference. Such a liberating climate should also enable them to become a little more self-confident, to become more realistic in their goals, to be more alert to new ideas, and hopefully to use different behaviors. If changed behavior is observed, then learning in its deepest and most meaningful sense has occurred.

Another powerful argument[10] for establishing an enhancing social-emotional climate in the learning situation involves its impact on society's purposes and value system. To some extent, American society and its machinery are geared toward preserving the status quo, so that groups of students, preordained for certain superior roles, are steered that way and labelled "the college bound." Other students are steered towards pre-ordained inferior statuses. If a psychological environment can be set up in a school or classroom such that it enables learners to re-examine, to explore, and to experiment, it will help to undermine some of this status quo*ism*. If our American heritage means anything, it ought to mean this. For when a learning situation is psychologically noncompartmentalized, open, and encouraging dialogue, interaction, and free-ranging examination of situations and procedures, then learners are liberated to inquire, to analyze, and to criticize. Most important, disadvantaged students may be enabled to make changes in their perceptions, in their roles and behaviors, and hence in their environment. Thus, "Disadvantaged children can escape poverty through the schools, they can escape hopelessness through the schools, they can also escape the ghetto through the schools. . . ."[11]

CONCLUSION

A liberating social-emotional climate deliberately created by acceptant and problem-oriented teachers can help enhance the learning of all students. Such a climate is particularly valuable for disadvantaged learners. By an analysis of teacher verbalizations through the use of the Social-Emotional Climate Index, teachers can begin to assess the learning climate in their own classrooms. Insofar as they produce a learner-centered kind of teaching-learning environment, they are able to enhance and facilitate the learning and problem solving of their students.

REFERENCES

1. George B. Brain, "Schools for Cities: The Problem of Urban Education," *The College of Education Record,* University of Washington, Vol. 32, No. 2, January 1966, p. 33.

2. N. A. Flanders, "Personal-Social Anxiety as a Factor in Learning" (unpublished doctoral dissertation, University of Chicago, 1949). Also, H. V. Perkins, "The Effects of Social-Emotional Climate and Curriculum on Learning of Inservice Teachers" (unpublished doctoral dissertation, University of Chicago, 1949). Also, Lucy Polansky, "Group Social Climate and the Teacher's Supportiveness of Group Status Systems," *Journal of Educational Sociology,* 1954.

3. Helen H. Jennings, "Leadership and Sociometric Choice," *Sociometry,* No. 10, 32-39, 1949. Also, Herbert A. Thelen, *Education and the Human Quest* (New York: Harper, 1960).

4. N. A. Flanders, *op. cit.;* also, N. A. Flanders, "Teacher Influence, Pupil Attitudes, and Achievement" (prepublication manuscript of a proposed research monograph, University of Michigan, Ann Arbor, 1962).

5. H. V. Perkins, *op. cit.*

6. Lucy Polansky, *op. cit.*

7. John Withall, "The Development of a Technique for the Measurement of Social-Emotional Climate in Classrooms," *Journal of Experimental Education,* 1949, p. 17. Also, John Withall, "Mental Health—Teacher Education Research Project," *Journal of Teacher Education,* September 1963.

8. John Withall, *Impact on Learners of Climate Created by the Teacher* (film), Bureau of Audio-Visual Instruction, University of Wisconsin, 1963.

9. Carl R. Rogers, "Significant Learning: In Therapy and in Education,"

Educational Leadership, January 1959. Also, Robert F. Mager, "On the Sequencing of Instructional Content," *Psychological Reports*, 9, Southern Universities Press, 1961. Also, A. W. Coombs, *The Professional Education of Teachers* (Boston: Allyn and Bacon, 1965).

10. Herbert A. Thelen, "Grouping Practices in Relation to Educational Ends and Means" (for the UNESCO Institute for Pedagogy, 1964).

11. George B. Brain, *op. cit.*, p. 37.

See also, Vernon Haubrich, "The Culturally Different: New Context for Teacher Education," *Journal of Teacher Education*, Vol. 14, No. 2, June 1963.

part **2**

ENGLISH—APPLICATIONS

Focus

Linguistics is frequently equated with the "new" English; it is seen in the same contexts as the "new" math and the "new" science; it is also seen, by those with a little knowledge of what the discipline entails, as the white hope for "correcting" the grammatical ills of the entire high school population and, in this context, it becomes a panacea that needs careful study.

At least three schools of linguistics can be identified: comparative, structural, and transformational. Of the three, structural and transformational are vying for supremacy within the English field; comparative linguistics, stressed more in the teaching of foreign languages, is not totally ignored by the other two schools, but it usually serves them in a supporting (generally historical) role.

Common to all three schools is the rationale for moving from prescriptive, that is, Latin-based traditional grammar, to structural analysis. Key ideas in this rationale are these: language is vocal; language symbols are arbitrary; language has system; language changes. With these and other like rubrics, linguistics removes the need for the most deadly of all English rituals, the grammar unit.

Most promising in this shift from prescriptive to descriptive grammar is the process or method used to help students arrive at testable generalizations about language. *Inductive teaching* is the professional concept for this process, and with its use English joins the sciences and mathematics in the newer techniques for studying traditional disciplines.

Linguistics as a structure-process for studying language promises much. Unfortunately, the process gets lost in most English classrooms where teachers concentrate on making students memorize a vocabulary as esoteric and useless as the old parts of speech. Nomenclature of the "new" grammar should be part of teachers' backgrounds but should seldom be inflicted on students in a junior or senior high school classroom. "Phoneme," "morpheme," and "suprasegmentals" may be useful for bright college bound students, but for the disadvantaged they are as useless as the advanced vocabulary of nuclear physics.

Instead, linguistic processes in classrooms of disadvantaged youth should concentrate on the implications of sounds as these sounds are identified in patterns; patterns, in turn, should be examined for meaning. Meaning should be analyzed with respect to given audiences—home, church, school, gang, hangout—with students studying the implications of behaviors elicited by given patterns with inappropriate audiences. Role playing of usage levels in context then becomes a means of identifying writing strategies. Where difficulties are encountered in such lessons, pattern drills, via tape recorders with individuals or with groups, should provide the practice needed to habituate a speech pattern necessary for economic survival. (Robert Pooley identified such survival usage patterns needed by anyone in contemporary American society in the December 1960 *NEA Journal*.)

How the foreign language teacher accomplishes the oral-aural teaching of language is described by Mr. Hallman with a view to possible adaptations by English teachers. Aspects of the language laboratory and its role in teaching English to disadvantaged youth should be checked out: whether the language laboratory uses a variety of tracks on its tapes and whether these tracked tapes can be used with conventional tape recorders. If all work is to be done in the laboratory, careful supervision of the students in their manipulation of controls is a *must*. If, on the other hand, tapes are to be used with conventional hardware within the English classroom with a small group or an individual, less supervision will be necessary.

Some of the language drills described by Mr. Hallman can also be put onto transparencies and the sight plus sound drills used simultaneously. As with any other method of teaching, content for drills, transparencies, dialogue substitutions, and the like should always come from the context of the students' activities.

Mr. Hallman outlines the potential for one breakthrough in teaching English to disadvantaged youth; teachers will have to use their local communities, their students' backgrounds, and their own ingenuity to make this nascent approach to the new grammar become an effective adjunct to the myriad that is English.

Linguistics and the Disadvantaged

CLEMENS L. HALLMAN

The problem of teaching English to the disadvantaged is closely related to the teaching of foreign languages in this country. Techniques used in teaching English as a second language to the culturally different (other ethnic background) and to the culturally deprived (substandard background) can be molded after those used today to teach a foreign language. We say "today" because the teaching of foreign languages in the United States has undergone a tremendous change in the last several years. Objectives, techniques, and instructional material have been almost completely revised. Much of this change has been due to findings and contributions of the fields of linguistics and psycholinguistics.

Approximately nineteen million individuals or 11 percent of the entire American population possessed a non-English mother tongue in 1960.[1] The English language to these culturally different is a second language, a *foreign* language that they are forced to learn in order to be socially acceptable. Likewise, English is a foreign language to the culturally deprived of our country. In both cases we have children whose native tongue and culture are acceptable until they reach school. At this time special problems are created because they are thrown into a large society. It is also at this time when a child's basic attitudes are formed; and the process of *acculturation,* which takes place as he leaves his preschool circle, will affect his whole life. The child discovers that something is different, that the teacher does not quite understand him. He often develops negative attitudes toward this new pressure and all that it represents. He may also reject the language and culture of his parents as inferior. All this results in a baffling and exasperating experience. In many cases he will be considered by the school as mentally subnormal or emotionally maladjusted and scholastically placed accordingly. This can also be the picture for the culturally deprived child who does not possess those experiences which form the base of our school's instructional materials. By no fault of his own he is placed into a society which talks a different dialect and refers to experiences which he does not possess. Such a difference may have been brought about by poverty, illiteracy, indifference of his elders, or just plain isolation. Children in both of these categories have been forced to change loyalties from one dialect and one culture to another.

In the United States we think that all cultures have fused into a great "melting pot." But this has not really taken place. We have tried to make all fit into a philosophical, linguistic, and cultural mold. Not long ago our government wanted the Indians to become part of our great culture so they separated the children from the influence of their parents by putting them into boarding schools and not allowing them to speak the language they had learned at home.[2] Fortunately, the experiment was not successful. Why do we try to *replace* the native (foreign or American) dialect with standard English? It is this author's point of view that we should *not* force the child to reject his nonstandard English as inferior or nonusable. What right do we have to impose our "superior" cultural pattern upon another? Who made the rules? What is "language" really? In most cases the child who learns the standard English in school will revert to the substandard at home. Let him do it! If we try to force him to forget and reject his substandard dialect, he will be considered as "putting on airs" by his family and old peers and will become an outcast. Chances are that at first he will not feel comfortable with those using the standard English either. A more reasonable solution would be to teach the standard English as a *second* dialect, attempting to have the child realize that he needs it in order to live and advance in the greater society. This can be done without forcing the child to reject his original dialect or culture. We have not been too successful in the United States in teaching standard English to the culturally different *or* the culturally deprived, so we do have a common problem. We have been least successful with the latter because we have assumed that their nonstandard English could serve as a basis for teaching standard English. Why not teach it as a second language? We have often assumed that we were teaching in a typical American school and have proceeded as we would have in Elkhart, Indiana or Harrisburg, Pennsylvania. We ignored the fact that English was not the first language of the children and that they were growing up as products of a totally different culture.

There are a number of studies concerning the theme of teaching English and bilingualism. Several of these are contained in a publication entitled "Non-Standard Speech and the Teaching of English."[3] In such a series, theory and practice are presented as related to attitudes towards nonstandard speech users. All articles express the conclusion that standard English should be taught as a second dialect and should be based upon the findings of linguistic science.

In the area of bilingualism the reader is referred to the March and April 1965 issues of *Modern Language Journal*.[4] The articles therein published were originally presented at the Conference for the Teacher of the Bilingual Child, University of Texas, June 8–10, 1964, under the direction of Dr. Joseph Michel. The whole gamit of bilingualism is discussed with an emphasis on ways and means of coping with the stigma attached to those whose first language is non-English.

LINGUISTIC IMPACTS

The organization of language is not based so much on logic as on the customs and conventions which are peculiar to each language. In English, for example, word order is very important; "the dog bit the boy" does not have the same meaning as "the boy bit the dog." One can also readily distinguish between boarding a bus in "he is taking a bus to New York" and hauling a bus in "he is taking a bus to New York." The way words are used and combined to make up larger units of speech such as phrases, clauses, and sentences is also of great importance. Since most utterances are made of clusters (nouns and verbs with their *satellites*, it is suggested that the student learn these as complete units. They are basic elements which constitute an utterance. They are units which should come to the speaker's mind already assembled and complete. Thus, the patterns of standard English need to be presented to the speaker of substandard English as *new* (and complete) utterances.

There are today some instructional materials for the teaching of foreign languages that are based on linguistic principles. As a result of a systematic comparison between two language systems, drills are prepared and presented giving due emphasis to the interference between the native and the target language. Underlying all this is the assumption that language consists primarily of speech patterns and that these are, for the most part, automatic for the native user.[5] Linguistics tells us that the learner of English as a second language must acquire (1) the basic features of the English sound system and (2) the basic features of English grammar and vocabulary. Materials which incorporate the above goals are available for foreign language teachers but are rather scarce for English teachers. Thus, at present, the English teacher is faced with a problem which is basically one of time. He can greatly benefit by having a basic knowledge of linguistics, but it would be inadvisable for him to produce his own material. Results of many who have attempted to do so are chaotic. Therefore, rather than trying to singlehandedly prepare material, he should know how to supplement traditional material (with patterns, visuals, etc.) until sound, linguistically based, instructional material becomes available.

Since language primarily consists of automatic speech patterns, we should strive to develop such a facility in the standard English in our culturally deprived as well as our culturally different. Patterns of standard English should be presented over and over until they become automatic. One should seek to:

(1) develop automatic responses to basic structural patterns, and

(2) concentrate on speaking before reading and writing.

In developing the above, teachers should remember that (1) grammatical rules should be descriptive and not prescriptive (summaries of behavior), and (2) comprehension and fluency require control of stress, intonation, and juncture in addition to other aspects of phonology.

TAPE DRILLS

One of the greatest aids to a language teacher is the mechanical device known as the tape recorder. With it he can use specially prepared tapes to introduce, drill, and reinforce instruction. Any material presented on tape should follow the same pattern as that prepared for classroom use. Unfortunately, many exercises undertaken in a tape laboratory will have no relationship whatsoever to what is being taught in the classroom. But what constitutes a good pattern? Let us attempt to suggest some pointers which apply to all drills, including those on tape.

(1) A pattern should emphasize a single problem. The drill should be built around one point of interference (between substandard and standard, native and foreign).

(2) The student should always know the purpose of the drill. It is suggested that the student be given an example of a pattern and of any expected modification he will be required to make. For example, if one is substituting *money* for *paper* in "I need paper," give the cue and show the student what change you want him to make and say, "I need money."

(3) The drill should be a complete utterance, a complete unit, for example, a noun or verb cluster.

(4) The drill should be as short as feasible. Do not add too many "trimmings" to your main point. A long utterance will bog down the learning process and confuse students.

(5) The drills should be designed for fast movement.

(6) The drills should be completely spoken. Remember, language is primarily speech.

(7) Drilling and testing should *not* be undertaken at the same time. Save the testing until after the students have learned the material.

(8) A taped pattern drill should provide a pause for student repetition followed by the correct response for reinforcement.

(9) Patterns should be presented in context, and the student should

be familiar with the context before the patterns are drilled. It is too much to expect a student to learn the vocabulary at the same time he is required to learn the mechanics of pattern change.

In selecting patterns for classroom or mechanical use (by means of a tape recorder or language laboratory) the teacher should first decide whether or not it will relate, reinforce, and complement instruction. It should not be a separate or an unrelated activity.

(1) What is the grammatical (or phonological) point involved?

(2) Is there a contrast between the two systems? Specifically, will the student encounter much intreference from his native language?

(3) What kind of pattern will lend itself best to this type of situation?[6]

Criteria for the selection of quality tape recordings have already been set up.[7] The profession is taking great interest in this new medium, and many valuable experiences have already been derived from it. Care should be taken, however, to ensure the quality as well as quantity of the tapes selected.

VISUALS

An important and often neglected aspect of second dialect learning lies in the area of relationship between objective reality and the acquisition of speech patterns. In English, as in any other language, there is direct association between reality, as seen by the native, and communication. Unless the nonnative is trained and exposed to such a direct association, he will resort to his native language system and try to bridge the gap. In doing so he uses the second dialect as a *second hand vehicle*.

Most of the new foreign language instructional materials do not provide for the above need, and as a result the learner does not really "command" the second language. The same situation holds for English materials used with children possessing substandard English. The learner must not only be exposed but drilled in the organization of thought of the particular second language. He should be made aware of the different way of organizing reality and should do exercises which focus attention on linguistic contrasts with which the speaker is not familiar.

Films, filmstrips, and other visual aids can play an important role in attempting to accomplish the above. They can serve as substitutes for the realities which the native speaker associates with language. In addition to such a role, they can aid in giving the student contrasts and various possibilities so that he can learn to make linguistic choices. Thus, visuals can serve as excellent cues in learning the patterns of the second dialect.

Some of the outstanding instructional programs use films in an at-

tempt to get the student to identify himself with the pictorial situation
he sees on the screen. Thus, the student establishes relationships between
groups of sounds and situations. He is forced to react to a given visual
situation along with the native language users on the screen. Such an
activity goes a long way in aiding the student to acquire a meaningful
command of a second language.

Visual aids and pattern drills can and should work hand in hand. A
quite interesting and promising innovation combines sound (tape reel or
cartridge) with a visual projection system. An example of such an aid is
the machine developed by John Carroll of Harvard University which
synchronizes a loop of magnetic tape with a 35 mm filmstrip loop projected on a small screen. Each combination of film and tape loop can be
presented three times (for previews, learning, and testing) but the number
and frequency of viewing are determined by the learner. Such a machine
not only combines the visual and the audio, but provides for self-pacing.

Although materials using visuals in an *integrated* program approach
have not as yet been produced in sufficient quantity, the trend in this
direction is definite and unmistakable. Teachers of standard English to
the culturally disadvantaged would be able to do a much more effective
job with such programs. Let us hope that this type of instructional material soon becomes available.

CONCLUSIONS

Many practices currently used in the area of teaching foreign languages could be incorporated into the teaching of English to disadvantaged
youth even though not all areas of language would present a one-to-one
"transplantability." Such would be the case for certain speakers of substandard English who may benefit to a greater degree from drills in the
area of syntax than drills in the area of phonology. The adaptability of
foreign language teaching procedures would thus depend on the range
of English substandardization. In any case, teachers of English to the
culturally disadvantaged should be encouraged to familiarize themselves
with techniques used by today's foreign language teachers as well as to
try to incorporate such techniques into their procedures. To do so, they
will need to adapt the philosophy and objectives of second language
teaching.

REFERENCES

1. Joshua A. Fishman *et al.*, "Language Loyalty in the United States." (A
mimeographed report, in three volumes, to the Language Research Section of
the United States Office of Education. Yeshiva University, New York, 1964.)

2. Chester C. Christian, Jr., "The Acculturation of the Bilingual Child," *Modern Language Journal*, Volume XLIX, No. 3, March 1965.

3. William A. Stewart (ed.), "Non-Standard Speech and the Teaching of English," Language Information Series 2, Center for Applied Linguistics of the Modern Language Association of America, 1755 Massachusetts Avenue N.W., Washington 36, D.C., 1964. Articles include: (a) "Foreign Language Teaching Methods in Quasi-Foreign Language Situations" by William A. Stewart, (b) "Non-Standard Negro Speech in Chicago" by Lee A. Pederson, (c) "Some Approaches to Teaching English as a Second Language" by Charlotte Brooks.

4. *The Modern Language Journal*, Robert F. Roeming (Managing Editor). Volume XLIX, Numbers 3 and 4, March and April 1965.

5. Clemens L. Hallman, "Pattern Drills for High School Use," *International Journal of American Linguistics* (Research Center in Anthropology, Folklore, and Linguistics, Indiana University, 1962).

6. For a detailed look at various types of language pattern drills, the reader is referred to the *Teacher's Manual of the Audio-Lingual Materials* (Harcourt, Brace, and World).

7. *MLA Selective List of Materials*, Modern Language Association of America, 4 Washington Place, New York, New York 10003, Appendix 2, 1962.

Focus

Reading is one of the largest baskets of snakes in contemporary American education. Everyone is an expert on the subject; it is regarded as the underlying cause of delinquency by a prominent New York City judge, as the basic tool for everything from nuclear physics to modern art by at least one Ph.D. in physics, and as the panacea for all the ills of education by many parents and commentators on education. Oddly enough, all these judgments may be correct in a given set of circumstances; but a statement by a scientist on the occasion of the Massachusetts Institute of Technology's Centennial Celebration in 1961 is perhaps most accurate: "Scientists just aren't sure how children learn to read." The scientist who made the statement was trying to help David Wayne, the narrator, explore the difference between a thinking machine and the human mind; the scientist's conclusion was that much more research was needed before answers to the question, "How do people learn to read?" could be given.

Yet, somehow, most people do learn to read, and schools build entire programs around the assumption that all students read. But Riessman and others who have studied the disadvantaged have identified the third grade as the fulcrum for reading's crucial role in the American school system. At that level, independent reading (outside assignments and the like) set up failure syndromes for marginal and nonreaders who, until that grade, have managed to survive.

That some students survive right into the junior high school is the topic of Professor Dunn's concern. Such students are in class because the law says that they must be there. With imagination and a knowledge of resources, English and Reading teachers can keep many disadvantaged students engaged in the struggle to improve their reading skills. While there are curricular innovations that can be used (these are discussed later), what Professor Dunn emphasizes are obvious blocks to reading interests that can presently be found in the schools. If schools and teachers were to follow her suggestions for overcoming these blocks and using some of the suggested resources, a step—but only a step—would be taken in stimulating disadvantaged readers' interests and, hopefully, their involvement with the printed word.

Reading and the Disadvantaged

ANITA E. DUNN

Clearly, too many Americans—children, adolescents, and adults—are reluctant readers, but one way to improve the desire to read is that which Mortimer Adler pointed out in *How to Read a Book*.

> When they [students] are in love and are reading a love letter, they read for all they are worth. They read every word three ways; they read between the lines and in the margins; they read the whole in terms of the parts, and each part in terms of the whole; they grow sensitive to context and ambiguity, to insinuation and implication; they perceive the color of words, the odor of phrases, and the weight of sentences. They may even take the punctuation into account. Then, if never before or after, they read.[1]

Adler's point—that material to be read should be personal, real, and important to the reader—requires that teachers, school and community librarians, youth counselors, and parents join other community leaders in combined attempts to identify materials which have the interest magnitude described by Adler. Where disadvantaged students are concerned such materials have been scarce in the past, but recent publishing innovations and funds from Title III of the Elementary and Secondary Education Act should provide the means for interested communities to acquire reading materials which will accommodate the reading interests of most disadvantaged students.

Project Head Start, funded to provide a reading readiness background for disadvantaged youth, cannot help the other million or so who have not had a head start in reading readiness. For some of these students, even at the junior high school level, it will mean beginning at the beginning to learn to read. Pulitzer Prize winner Harrison Salisbury described the dilemma when he pointed out:

> It is hard for many of us to imagine how narrow the world must be for youngsters who cannot read well enough to study elementary les-

sons let alone literature, history, poetry, or philosophy. Yet hundreds of thousands of teenagers are growing toward adulthood with minds which are crippled by their inability to unlock the key to the printed page.[2]

Conant also cites the importance of an all-out attack on the reading problems of disadvantaged youth:

> In the slum school the development of reading is obviously of first importance. The earlier the slow readers are spotted and remedial measures instituted, the better.[3]

Some tactics have already proved successful in encouraging reading among disadvantaged students. Specially trained children's librarians, summer reading programs, and the Junior Great Book discussions are having some impact. With their classroom displays of inviting books, their reading aloud to children, and their skillful teaching techniques, kindergarten, primary, and elementary school teachers have also improved the reading tastes of many youngsters.

In spite of these improvements there yet remains the adolescent who has been unable to establish reading as a pleasurable and rewarding habit, and his numbers are legion. Somewhere along the line, children who almost inherently want to learn to read become reluctant or nonreading adolescents. For them, reading has become a drudgery, not a delight. One wonders what occurred to turn these children from readers to reading-allergic adolescents and, later, to nonreading adults?

THE PROBLEM

One source of answers to this question may be students' comments about assigned reading tasks: "I hate books." "I don't like to read." "We ain't got no books at home." "Reading's hard." "It takes too much time." "I'd rather watch TV." "In school, they won't let ya read the books or magazines ya like." "There ain't any good books in the library; just stuff teachers make ya read."

School policy when applied to the shelving of books, to the selection of reading materials, to study hall procedures, and the like sometimes serves to deter student reading. Some specific examples of these and other rituals as they tend to inhibit student reading are as follows.

(1) Shelving teen-agers' and children's books in the same section of the library is not an appealing arrangement for adolescents who consider themselves almost adults.

(2) Crowding books especially written for adolescents in with an overwhelming collection of adult books is equally unacceptable. The already book-wary young shy away from such an arrangement.

(3) Prohibiting youngsters and teen-agers from reading books and magazines in classrooms, study halls, and homerooms is a real deterrent to reading encouragement.

(4) Neglecting to provide periodically a regularly scheduled class period to read library books misses a chance to develop a reading desire. In too many classrooms, no time is planned for young people to go to the library to select books to read. No provision is made to spend a class hour occasionally in the library. All young people, but especially the disadvantaged youth, need a proper reading climate, a quiet place to read.

(5) Frowning on the books young people select to suit their tastes stifles their reading interest. "They should all read the classics"—not eventually, but now—ready or not. In one instance, an English teacher sent a reluctant reader back to the library to select another book because the girl's choice, *Let the Hurricane Roar* (a worthy piece of literature), was in the teacher's opinion "just a thin book." Would we have called *Lord Jim* "just a thin book?"

(6) Lacking knowledge about books written for young people handicaps teachers in assisting students to find books they will enjoy. Books—good books—which will whet the appetite of the reluctant reader are plentiful. Too many teachers still regard all books written expressly for teen-agers as *trashy* reading material. For the disadvantaged youth, books such as *Hot Rod, South Town, Shuttered Windows, Knock at the Door, Emmy, Roosevelt Grady, Mary Jane, Skid, Joe-Pole,* and *A Present for Rosita* are excellent stepping stones on the path to reading.

(7) Failing to provide classroom libraries of attractive books, magazines, and newspapers loses an opportunity to stimulate the habit of reading. Teachers of the disadvantaged need to remember that accessibility is one of the prerequisites for the encouragement of reading. By using the attractive, worthwhile *Literature Sampler* in the classroom, teen-agers may be enticed to read books via their contact with excerpts which have been tested for adolescent appeal.

(8) Hesitating to read stories or parts of books aloud cheats children and young adults of a pleasurable and necessary aural reading experience. Disadvantaged youths, especially, have missed much because no one has ever read to them.

Reading aloud from carefully selected books that will interest a particular grade level is an almost unbeatable technique for encouraging reading. *Call it Courage, Old Yeller, Bristle Face, A Quiet Hero, Shane, Mrs. 'Arris Goes to Paris,* and others with fast moving plots and abundant conversation are suitable for oral interpretation and are sure-fire starters. Books lists such as *Fare for the Reluctant Reader, Gateways to Readable Books, Good Books for Poor Readers, Reading Ladders for Human Re-*

lations, and *Your Reading* suggest many other books and magazines for young people who are usually not interested in reading.

SUGGESTIONS

(1) Keep school libraries open throughout the year to serve as community libraries or to supplement the local library. "Schools must become community centers, providing welfare and social services as well as learning" was one of the major conclusions reached by the 1965 White House Conference on Education.

A survey of the public library facilities and services in a city of about 120,000 people in eastern New York State revealed a regrettable condition. Only one library set aside one small room for young adults. That room was labelled "Young People's Room." The children's and young people's libraries in that city were closed most evenings and all day Saturday during the summer, the season when young people have the most leisure time.

(2) Hire boys and girls to work in the library—especially disadvantaged youth. At first, the young hired help could assist in the library workroom. One of their first jobs might be removing the due dates from some of the books. This is one date that frightens the almost nonreader. He needs more time to read his book.

These aides can be trained to charge out books, check in books, and shelve books. Some disadvantaged students can be taught to compile teen-age book lists. They can enlist the aid of the teen-ager who finally found a book he liked to read. The young readers can write brief opinions about their favorite books.

Tape recorders could be made available in the library, and the disadvantaged youth could record his remarks. Such a tape recorded comment would be a fine project for girls enrolled in secretarial courses to transcribe. Pile a stack of these weekly or monthly "best seller" lists in prominent places in the school or community library and label them: "Take one; they're for you."

(3) Erect a library building or add an annex to the community library exclusively for these young adults—a teen-age "reading hangout." Young people like to go where the gang goes. Why not have the gang gather in a teen-age library? The "gang" concept will gradually change to "club," but the youths must make this thought transition themselves. An attractively and comfortably furnished teen-age Utopian Library would match and surpass the lure of the corner newsstand.

(4) Arrange books in a teen-age "Utopia" in a supermarket and bookstore style. Why must the books in too many libraries for children and young adults be arranged only or mainly by the Dewey Decimal System

(DDS), a system designed by a librarian for the ease and convenience of trained librarians? It is surely not a system designed for the ease and convenience of adolescents, especially disadvantaged youth. They are not interested in DDS. They cannot remember the classifications. Why should they? Such a system is too time consuming and too confusing. Later, when these young people have become mature readers, they can learn to use the card catalog and the Dewey Decimal System in the adult section of the library. Borrow some of the salesmanship techniques of the supermarket. These pressure salesmen display books under clearly readable signs: Mysteries, Sports, Hobbies, Cookbooks. They put up front what they want to sell. Try such selling techniques in the young adult library. Shelve all the sports books in one area. Youthful artists can prepare clever signs, cartoons, and posters that point the way to the kinds of books boys want to read. Compete with and outsell the lurid true romance magazines. Prominently display books for girls on love and romance, on beauty hints, and on the *She-Manners*.

Print the last names of teen-age author idols on fairly large signs—Felsen, Sperry, Meader, Stolz, Means. Headline the section: "Here they are; books by your favorite authors."

Arrange a special section of attractive editions of more adult books for the mature reader such as *Red Badge of Courage, Kon-Tiki*, and *Moby Dick*. Call attention to these titles via Francis Bacon: "Some books are to be tasted, others to be swallowed, and some few to be chewed and digested. . . ."[4]

(5) Man Teen-age "Utopia" with some male librarians especially trained to handle young adults. Boys who are reluctant readers and almost nonreaders need a man who can comment. "That's a good book. You'll like it. I read it."

(6) Follow the fine example set by the Henry Hormer Boys Clubs in Chicago and add a well-stocked reading room to Boys' Clubs, Girls' Clubs, Catholic youth societies, and other youth organizations. Citizens of the community could contribute the magazines, paperbacks, and books to these youth centers. Once there, teen-agers could be encouraged to take them home—no strings attached. These magazines, books, and paperbacks are theirs to keep or to pass on. Some donated magazines and paperbacks could also be placed on shelves in employment offices for adolescents and their parents.

(7) Display book jackets in prominent places in the school: on the first floor bulletin board, in the classrooms, in the cafeteria, and even in the locker rooms. Lay a Hansel and Gretal trail to the library. Trophies awarded for athletic prowess and physical fitness hold a place of honor

and prominence. Why not reading fitness awards, trophies, and compensations?

(8) Advertise and review books for young adults in the local newspaper on the sports page, in the comic section, or in a unique column devoted exclusively to teen-agers and young adults. Such announcements of popular adolescent literature will more than pay dividends in selling reading to youth. Local editors and merchants might be willing to underwrite the cost of so worthy an advertisement. Hawaii's *Honolulu Advertiser* added a special Sunday supplement entitled "Hawaii's Youth," written and edited primarily by teen-agers themselves, which included reviews of new books.

(9) Park bookmobiles next to the children's playground, the Little League field, the sand-lot baseball diamond, the teen-age hangouts, or the shopping center. Man these vehicles, too, with competent teen-age reading specialists to help encourage reading interests among the disadvantaged.

(10) Provide a reading clinic as part of every community library to supplement reading clinics in school! Developmental and remedial reading skills could be taught to disadvantaged youngsters, adolescents, and adults in an atmosphere surrounded by books, in a place conducive to nourishing the desire to learn to read well. The following opinion of Edwin and Marie Smith stresses the necessity of improving the reading ability of many Americans.

> Americans buy more books and newspapers than any other peoples of the world, yet a great many Americans read less than a book a year. This curious condition has come about because many Americans have difficulty in reading with ease and pleasure. Some, of course, cannot read at all. Skill in reading is perhaps the single most important intellectual skill needed by everyone today. Radio and television are effective means of spreading news quickly, but they cannot and will not replace the persistent everyday need for the ability to read with ease and understanding.[5]

(11) Heed the appeal of the paperbacks. Set up a paperback stand in the young adult library, in the school library, and in the classroom library, or promote a teen-age paperback bookstore in the school. Use the Teen-age Book Club of the Scholastic Magazine Corporation to start a classroom collection of paperbacks. Make it possible to purchase paperbacks at a cheaper rate than the newsstand and supermarket competitors. Hire a teen-ager or let students handle the paperback stand or store. Every young person should be enabled once in his life to own his own book. For every four paperbacks or books a young adult reads and on which he has recorded or written a brief comment, he might be awarded a free copy. In this way he can begin to build his own personal library.

NEXT STEPS

This article has suggested possible steps for encouraging reading among adolescents, especially among disadvantaged youth. Parents, teachers, librarians, and community leaders can apply some of the suggestions. Appeals to other local, state, and national political figures to join the effort should be a next step for expanding reading horizons. Ask for their support—socially, morally, and financially. In the past, America has failed to provide enough money for educating its youth. But today, both Titles I and III of the Elementary and Secondary Education Act provide generous funds for the implementation of imaginative reading programs, programs that augur well for the reading skills needed by the disadvantaged.

REFERENCES

1. Mortimer J. Adler, *How to Read a Book* (New York: Simon and Schuster, 1940), p. 14.

2. Harrison E. Salisbury, *The Shook-Up Generation* (Greenwich, Connecticut: Fawcett Publications, Inc., 1958), p. 117.

3. James Bryant Conant, *Slums and Suburbs* (New York: McGraw-Hill Book Co., 1961), p. 23.

4. Robert U. Jameson, *Essays Old and New* (New York: Harcourt, 1955), pp. 8-10.

5. Edwin H. and Marie P. Smith, *Teaching Reading to Adults* (Washington, D.C.: National Association of Public School Adult Educators, 1962), p. 7.

Focus

The success of O. K. Moore in teaching reading and writing to preschool students via "talking" typewriters and other hardware for getting students involved with learning experiences is but a prelude to what cyberneticians regard as a kind of millenium for the teaching of composition: the day when composition becomes an elective in a school curriculum. That such a day is coming is the confident prediction of communication experts such as Claude Shannon, Warren Weaver, and the late Norbert Wiener. Direct image transmission from brain to brain or machine to brain via amplification of electrical impulses already identified within the brain will be the vehicle for achieving this phenomenon.

There is no group in the American educational system that would welcome this breakthrough in the teaching of composition more than disadvantaged rural youth. Their problems of reading, speaking, and listening are minor compared to the sheer hatred they express for writing assignments. What English teacher has not heard the question, "How long?" or "How many words should it [the composition] be?" And after the tortuous prose has been set down by the disadvantaged student (with a miserly attention to word count), what teacher has not had the embarrassment of seeing a student crumple a returned composition with its time consuming suggestions for improvement into an amorphous ball of scrap without so much as a second glance at the carefully worded marginalia?

Sometimes (as Mrs. Graham implies in the article that follows) such student behavior may be justified. Her implied justification for students' negative behavior pivots upon the need for compositions to be based on students' interests and experiences. Disadvantaged students need something to write about, something that "grabs" them; yet most writing assignments given to the disadvantaged have all the interest of a pile of sawdust. Strategies for utilizing topics and experiences that interest disadvantaged youth are described in detail in the article which follows and provide a rationale for composition as a needed and useful experience for all disadvantaged youth, until the millenium described above becomes the *modus vivendi* for curricular structures. That needed skills in organization, clarity, and logic can be taught in classrooms of disadvantaged youth under the rubric of composition is Mrs. Graham's conviction, and her examples powerfully support this idea.

Composition and the Disadvantaged

THEODORA R. GRAHAM

To a culturally disadvantaged student, English class frequently epitomizes the ordered conceptual world where fine words and genteel manners seem to cover a "mess" of strong emotions and quick reactions. Here he is introduced to the "correct" way of using a language which has already served him rather well in its "incorrect" form. Perhaps he is told unequivocally that "good" speech and writing are essential keys to the world of jobs and pay increases and to a steady existence in which desires are regularly realized.

If a young person from a depressed area can still be touched at ages 14 through 17 by such appeals—if, that is, he is not already alienated from the cultural values that dominate the success scene—he soon discovers that their acceptance confronts him with major discrepancies in his perception of his small world. Learning English is like learning a foreign language,[1] and he finds himself shifting back into speech which seems less artificial once he leaves English class. What writing he does—about "My Mother," "My Favorite Place," "Our Trip to X-town"—is the result of almost physical pain, often rewarded by endless red notations around misspelled words and alongside punctuation errors, neither of which he will master in any appreciable way by the year's end.

The English classroom itself is boring (or worse, stifling) to a boy or girl who wants to be on the go, for its activities are sedentary and cerebral. Primary emphasis is placed on reading ability and quick perception of relationships, two skills research has shown are minimally developed in many disadvantaged students.[2] By the high school years, the stumbling over and guessing of elementary school have merged into comments such as: "Don't ask me"; "I don't know"; "What's this for, anyway?"; "This is a waste of time."

No wonder then that composing an essay seems like some exotic rite performed only by initiates, or like the wooden routine of getting enough words down to fill one page. For a student who has difficulties with "accepted" language, hearing once again about his inadequacy will not help. Believing, moreover, that his experiences are too commonplace to matter or too "tough" to put before the teacher's eyes, he may withdraw himself from the act of writing, giving the teacher what he thinks she wants or simply "forgetting" to do homework.

THE FOCUS

Here then is the well-known dilemma. Nevertheless, I submit that the only excuse for an impoverished English class for culturally disadvantaged students is impoverished imagination on both teaching and administrative levels. For where there is a genuine concern and imagination, teachers chuck clichés about drill, practice, and tight control—all ploys which have fostered dull days of endless repetition—and begin to perceive students as their counterparts in a human relations framework. Important factors emerge from what had seemed like a hopeless morass when two basic questions are confronted: (1) "What do I know about these students and the ways in which each is individually different from any other learner?" and (2) "What must be the priorities in this particular English class?"

Although my focus is upon composition, it is immediately apparent that before anything can be done to improve the soil for this activity, many tenaciously held ideas about what constitutes English must be plowed under. Unfounded assumptions and generalities—if they don't read Shakespeare here, they'll never read him; if they don't learn to spell, they won't get anywhere; if their speech habits don't improve, they'll be stuck in "that" neighborhood forever—cannot be permitted to provide the impetus for planning curriculum. Desks and chairs bolted to the floor must not dictate the limits of classroom activities and techniques. Unwillingness to disturb quiet hallways, to hold a "coffee" (or "coke") when guest speakers visit, to move the English teacher into the metal shop, the distributive education preparation sessions, the office practice room, or the social studies class—*instead* of moving the class to the teacher—will, I am sure, change into encouragement when priorities are re-examined.

PRIORITIES

In light of these considerations, I propose several general priorities which are based on what can now be stated or projected about the present and future world the disadvantaged youth must confront. English class must provide:

(1) experiences which will expand the student's perception both in situational width and in critical depth;

(2) opportunities to discover his adequacy to deal with ideas and feelings and to translate his chagrin, disappointment, or disillusion into positive action that matters to *him;*

(3) understanding that language is a tool which can be used differently depending upon the user's intent;

(4) knowledge that ordering and structuring are the means of controlling what may at first appear confusing and unmanageable.

From a very young age, a child of a moderately happy middle-class home grows gradually in each of these four categories; his successes in school reinforce his ability to cope with increasingly complex situations. The disadvantaged child, on the other hand, through numerous harsh encounters, seems to leap toward maturity while finding his ability to cope with complexity thwarted by the school. As Martin Deutsch points out, "The frustration inherent in not understanding, not succeeding, and not being stimulated in the school, although being regulated by it, creates a basis for the further development of negative self-images and low evaluations of individual competencies."[3]

With these priorities foremost in mind, what kinds of attitudes and activities can be built into revamped English programs that will stimulate the student and lead to writing as a natural outgrowth of experience?

APPLICATIONS

First, the teacher must acknowledge more than tacitly a firmly established fact about language: there is no single set of "correct" principles which dictate usage. Once students feel that saying "doesn't" instead of "don't" after "he" is wholly a matter of choice and situation, their common reaction, "Nobody talks like that," will change to a more accurate statement, "Nobody around where I live talks like that, but many people in this school and on television do." If the reaction is expanded to "I could talk like that if I wanted to—and could remember how he used those words," a major step towards awareness of what constitutes language difference has been taken.

Second, the concept of English as a subject or separate life activity must be recognized as invalid, not just in introductory talks on the first day of class, but throughout the entire curriculum for disadvantaged students. Though studying literature as art is a special focus, and one from which writing instruction can and should evolve, most writing must be related to concrete activities which the student finds practical and worthwhile. This can occur in English class itself or, as previously suggested, in other classes where discussion and writing emerge as necessary parts in a larger endeavor. If the results of learning can indeed be seen in behavior changes, then it is the teacher's responsibility to provide experiences in which such changes can occur with a minimum of frustration.

Thus, I am suggesting that English both fuse and diffuse, and that in certain well-selected cases writing be the culmination of an immediate or extended experience. Several examples may illustrate what I mean by diffusion and, hopefully, may suggest numerous other possibilities.

With the cooperation of shop, clerical, distributive education, and home management colleagues, the English teacher can become a resource person, devising ways to teach spelling of technical terms by using chapters from specialized textbooks and magazines (from *Hair-Do* to *Popular Mechanics*), to improve reading skills, or to help students plan the advertising and program for a skills show. Student paragraphs describing a self-made outfit, a metal sculpture, the process of refinishing a chair or developing a photograph, and methods of keeping tools in good condition can become part of dittoed handbooks distributed at school assemblies or on parents' night. If teachers in other areas credit and reinforce the value of these activities, students who otherwise refuse to write can find satisfaction and reward for practical and worthwhile activity.

Extremely important in such projects is the English teacher's approach to students' first efforts, for in the beginning some pupils will need samples to discuss, skeleton models to follow, and suggestions from classmates about how accurate and understandable their paragraphs are. Here are opportunities for minimal criticism from the teacher. Further, students' comments can be carefully channeled toward what is important, what people will want to know. In a school where flexibility is welcomed in every class, typing students can then make up first draft editions for each paragraph (including spelling and punctuation errors) which in turn will be cooperatively checked by the student and the teacher to determine needed improvements. At this point the teacher may act as an expert consultant rather than a grader or determiner of rightness. Some paragraphs will be mere lists of simple sentences; others will lack vividness. For a start, however, they will offer varying levels of success to a class of individuals sharing a group project.

Other examples of diffusion illustrate an essential fact about students who regularly shun standardized English classes: variety, immediacy, and spontaneity must become principles in planning. The weekly syllabus passed down year after year will have to go the way of all worn-out tools. This will provide room for short, experience-centered units capitalizing on the students' interests and abilities. With the help of a social studies teacher, a unit on controversial issues can be started in that class, work its way into the community, back into the school through speakers selected by the students, into heated open discussion among students, and culminate in a brief essay stating the writer's final view. Pressing issues sure to involve students about to enter the labor market are social security, health and medical insurance, union benefits, draft regulations, auto safety, and a long-awaited community project. What sixteen year old wouldn't be willing to try to write a safety versus design analysis of his favorite car?

Community involvement is particularly important for young people who often feel outside the mainstream of all but neighborhood life. Asking community leaders—businessmen, doctors, lawyers, salesmen, town officials—what they think about the above issues may initially seem an awesome and even impossible task. Again, the teacher's attitudes and approach must reassure the students that as a worker, consumer, and voter he will have the responsibility and right to ask questions. Furthermore, what the student will be able to write as a result of his curiosity and research will doubtless impress him. A writing assignment developed on the theme of "what I knew before I started and what I know now" can pinpoint increased perception.

DESIGNS

Another kind of fusion—one currently taking place in humanities classes—can easily and perhaps more fruitfully occur in units interspersed with those described above. In idea-centered units—like Men and Machines, What Is Entertainment?, Where Did Jazz (or Rock 'n Roll) Come From?—activities can be as simple or varied as individual ability in a class permits. Admittedly, planning for such units requires hours of selecting, taping, and mimeographing a wide variety of materials. In ninth grade, "Men and Machines" might include the following.

A Unit Design

William Carlos Williams, "The Red Wheelbarrow"
Mark Twain, "Old Times on the Mississippi" (description of the steamboat's arrival)

Film: Pacific 231
Emily Dickinson, "I Like to See It Lap the Miles"
Walt Whitman, "To a Locomotive"
Wilbur Schramm, "Dan Peters and Casey Jones"
William Saroyan, "Locomotive 38, the Ojibway"

John Updike, *The Centaur* (description of garage grease-pit)
Wilbur Schramm, "Windwagon Smith"
Karl Shapiro, "Auto Wreck"

Carl Sandburg, "The New Farm Tractor"
Stanley Kunitz, "The War Against the Trees"
Peter Blake, *God's Own Junkyard*

Katherine B. Shippen, "Kitty Hawk"
Robert P. Tristram Coffin, "First Flight"
Wolfgang Langewiesche, "Why an Airplane Flies"
Newspaper material on auto styles, machinist strike, or other relevant articles

John Updike, "A & P" (Sammy's reaction to cash registers)
Leroy Anderson, "The Typewriter Song"
Carl Sandburg, "Manual System"
Caroline E. Emerson, "The Ups and Downs of the Elevator Car"
Film: The Awesome Servant

Magazine hunt: articles about "What Machines Do," future uses of computers, and automation in office and factory
Popular Science, Popular Mechanics
Advertisements and machines: increasing demands for hair dryers, can openers, dish washers, latest model cars, "hi-fi" stereos

Louis B. Saloman, "Univac to Univac"
Computer-composed music
Isaac Asimov, "It's Such a Beautiful Day"
Rudyard Kipling, "The Secret of the Machines"
Selected painting and sculpture

Listening to Updike describe a grease-pit or cash register, Kunitz depict a bulldozer, or Shapiro recall an ambulance and wrecked car may touch off prose-poems in subjects some students would never have imagined worthy of poetry. Others may be more interested in comparing farming, mining, or household equipment used in countries at various levels of development. Older pupils are deadly serious about automation and how it may affect their future as job hunters. Writing a letter of application or filling out forms to order parts and equipment become integrated activities, not isolated, meaningless chores.

In designing such a unit as "What Is Entertainment?" the teacher commands almost endless possibilities for reading, speaking, writing, and acting. (Students who ordinarily balk at reading "serious" drama can still enjoy viewing a carefully chosen Shakespearean scene whose parts are read by a practiced resident company within the class.) Central to the activities planned by the teacher must be a desire to bring students into a critical confrontation both with what they *like* and with new entertainment experiences. What is "soul" music, and who can understand it? What if television were to vanish forever? Can anyone really do anything about

programs and advertising besides turning the sound down? Does television
or radio entertainment cost anything? Do fun and laughter have to be the
results of what we call entertainment?

SUMMARY

Given room to test opinions, prejudices, and feelings about these
questions in open class discussion, where chairs are arranged in a large
oval or rectangle with the teacher as one participant, the student can
move at the right moment to ordering and developing ideas on paper.
If, in the charged atmosphere of a classroom alive with ideas important
to him, the ordinarily uninvolved or unmoved student is ready to fight
verbally for his views, then for him the self-commitment demanded of
any honest writer becomes a real choice. Such occasions may be infre-
quent: one successful paragraph or short essay could rightfully be the
only structured writing experiences during a four-week unit. But the
teacher attuned to the needs of disadvantaged youth and concerned with
genuine priorities will know that, unlike mechanical once-a-week compositions, his students' experiences with writing count in the development
of meaningful individual expression.

REFERENCES

1. Ruth I. Golden, "Slow Learners—Instructional Tapes and Insight," *The
English Journal*, **51**, 418-420, 442, September 1962.

2. Benjamin S. Bloom, Allison Davis, and Robert Hess, *Compensatory
Education for Cultural Deprivation* (New York: Holt, Rinehart, and Winston,
1965). See multiple research studies, pp. 50-52.

3. Martin Deutsch, "The Disadvantaged Child and the Learning Process,"
Education in Depressed Areas, A. Harry Passow (ed.), Teachers College,
Columbia University, New York, 1963, p. 177.

Focus

"Collage" has set more editorial assistants to shaking their heads than anyone can imagine. Polite ones strike out the *a*, stick in an *e*, and say nothing. W. Wilbur Hatfield's secretary back in 1951 complained to him that as then editor of *The English Journal* it was a shame that an English teacher could not even spell "college." Keen, as he still is today, Mr. Hatfield asked the secretary to look up the word in the dictionary whereupon, red-faced, she curbed further comments until she thoroughly checked them out in some standard reference. By this time readers, used to swift absorption of content, are aware that "collage" is not "college" and that deliberate use of the word with the *a* and its total aura is intended.

Collage as a teaching technique in classrooms of disadvantaged youth is both a structure and a process; it is not a panacea, but it is one way to exemplify how all the foregoing perceptions from numerous disciplines can be focused on a single learning experience. Whether readers espouse the cause of the language arts, the tripod, or both they will find in the article applications of principles taken from students' psychological, sociological, English, reading, listening, composition, and other backgrounds.

Important as the collage is as Gestalt and teaching technique, it is sometimes vitiated by teachers who claim that their disadvantaged students would *never* sit still for such a presentation. These teachers argue that their students are (1) too numerous, (2) too limited in ability, and (3) too undisciplined to go through such an experience. While such teachers' arguments may be valid, the group described in the following article is a class of ninth graders at a reform school. Their average I.Q. is 85; they range in age from 15 to 21, and they number 32. Any one of these students in a public high school according to their police records would be capable of putting a regular classroom into a state of complete chaos. If they seem unusually attentive or docile as described in the following article, keep in mind that they were *interested* in what was going on; they were *involved* in the problem being studied, and they had a variety of *alternatives* for presenting their viewpoints. Most important, their views

83

were regarded by the teacher as *important* and *worthy* of serious consideration.

Some readers of the article may claim that the collage as a technique does not further students' understanding of T. S. Eliot's "objective correlative." Agreed, but when one considers that half of these boys were incarcerated because they hated school so much that they were classified as habitual truants, justification for the collage technique in teaching English to them would seem to be established on what is known as face validity.

Finally, no one claims that the use of the collage technique, or any other technique for that matter, will turn reluctant students into avid scholars; in fact, if 15 percent of a given class of disadvantaged students catch the "scholastic faith," it will be a remarkable accomplishment. As pointed out in the Introduction, by the time most disadvantaged youth get to high school they accept failure as their lot in life; they have, in most cases, given up. But some of them are salvageable, and some of those who do "catch the faith" go on to become outstanding in their field. It is for those few and for the others who must know, if only darkly, that teachers are concerned about their future involvement in society that disadvantaged youth cannot and should not be relegated to a limbo of unteachables. If, as teachers, we can get across the idea to them that we think what they say is important, to that extent will they develop a concern for—even a confidence in—their later decision making in an increasingly complex society.

Literature and the Disadvantaged

EDWARD R. FAGAN

Given a set of outdated textbooks which must be used and a ninth-grade group of 32 boys who range in age from 15 to 21, who range in I. Q. from 85 to 140, whose ethnic composition is 75 percent nonwhite (Indian and Negro), and whose hatred of school is documented via police records of habitual truancy, what teaching strategies can be used to keep these students interested enough in learning to prevent them from making the classroom a battleground?

That was the question I faced some years ago when I accepted the task of teaching English, grades 9 through 12, to boys in a Wisconsin reform school. The lessons I learned during my two year stay at that school have never been forgotten and have been applied to both high school and college classes to good advantage over the last fifteen years. When I use "to good advantage," I mean that the students at both the high school and college levels increased their awareness of English as a discipline and frequently changed their attitude about education from negative to positive.

These lessons learned the hard way, let me repeat for the sake of the purists, did increase students' skill in English. Content was not "watered down." Students did not "play games," and the teacher did not "stoop to the students' level" in the derogatory sense of these expressions. Rather, students increased English skills as measured by standardized tests in the subject (California, Iowa) and shifted from negative to positive vectors concerning education, again as measured by attitude scales. Further, such judgments were not made by the author or by the reform school, but by members of a visiting team from the Wisconsin State Education Department.

This article will attempt to describe the structures and the processes by which these changes occurred, in the hope that the modest success achieved with such an "uneducable group" may encourage teachers with possibly more tractable, but certainly disadvantaged, groups to develop similar techniques for their work in English classrooms throughout the nation.

THE SETTING

Under the heading "English–Grade 9," the syllabus at the reform school contained the usual general objectives: "To increase students' skills in reading, writing, speaking, and listening; to expand students' vocabulary and spelling; to review basic grammatical principles," etc. Under the "Materials" section were the usual textbooks (one for grammar, one for literature), workbooks, standardized tests, audio-visual aids, and the like. As in many schools, the syllabus was hopefully designed as a blueprint, with the expectation that teachers would use skill and imagination in adapting the design to help students achieve the program's goals. Supplementary materials were at hand—commercial exercises for teaching uses of the *Readers' Guide,* dittoed spelling lists, and commercial book lists by grade levels. Recognizing that standard workbooks would be virtually useless with these students, I had prepared, in addition to the materials described above, dittoed Study Guides for each unit of the literature and grammar texts. These Study Guides used contents based on local events in such a way that they reinforced concepts and principles which the textbook identified as being important.

Into the Plan Book I inscribed: "Unit I: Language and Literature." Ambitiously, I listed unit objectives, described articulated homework assignments built around a variety of language arts skills (reading, writing, grammar, spelling, and vocabulary, which were directly related to materials that preceded and followed the daily work), and planned frequent quizzes to test students' learning. One might almost call the unit a methods textbook model of what *ought to be.* As an "authority" on high school English, I felt that the contents and the procedures used were my professional prerogative and that I could prescribe exactly what the students should "cover."

At the end of a week which might aptly be described as a disaster, I tried to analyze what had happened. My thinking went something like this: both the content and the procedures used were relatively typical of any high school class, so, for those students who were in the reform school because of truancy, the class was simply an enforced imposition of rituals which they had hated from the sixth grade on.[1] Secondly, I assumed (incorrectly) that I had a truly captive audience and that the sheer boredom of institutional life would guarantee that their homework assignments would be done. Another assumption along the same lines was that discrepancies in reading skills would be compensated for by the large block of study time that students would have back in their cottages. Hence, students who had only sixth-grade reading skills would take an extra half-hour or hour to struggle through the ninth-grade textbook material. As any experienced English teacher knows, such student dedication to reading is the exception rather than the rule. Finally, though the dittoed Study Guides proved interesting to the students, no transfer of content from the guides to the assigned materials took place. As a capstone to these thoughts, I concluded that I had been a "readin', writin' " teacher in the same old stereotype, and that if I ever wanted to get through to these students I had better come up with something different—and in a hurry.

THE PROCEDURE

If print would not work as a means of catching the students' attention, or if the students, for one reason or another, refused to get involved with print as a medium of education, then something which would get them to use the senses not yet inhibited by the formalities of English, something which would give them a sense of participation in the world around them, had to be tried. Such a nondiscursive medium was found in the collage. Now, a collage (the term is borrowed from art) is an organization of materials to form a design—in this instance, to express an idea. To explore the possibilities of this device, two films, *Picture in Your Mind* and *Boundary Lines*, were shown.[2]

Picture in Your Mind had the following thesis: world cooperation is possible if prejudice conceived in ignorance is removed by an educational process. The outstanding feature of the film was the various symbols it used to sustain the above message. Like the theme in a great symphony, the circle (a symbol of the inclusion of all mankind) appeared in some form in every scene. Harmonizing with this theme was the growth theme. The growth of a seed to a flower, the growth of an ovum to a human, the growth of a tribe to a society, all these and more were presented to symbolize the tremendous time factors, common patterns, and cooperative efforts involved in the growth of civilization.

Boundary Lines had the same theme as *Picture in Your Mind*—world cooperation. The "lines" part of the title is based on the fact that specific lines convey specific ideas. For instance, in cartoons and comics loudness is expressed by a series of vertical and horizontal lines around the mouth and head area of the cartoon character. Dizziness and intoxication are indicated by tight spirals over the head of a victim. Wavy lines indicate water, while rising jagged lines indicate mountains. This example of line symbol (taken directly from the first part of the film) is preparatory to taking the audience one step further with the postulate that a line may also be an idea, for example, the color line between races. The color line in such a case may become a division line. This division line the film superimposes on a globe of the world, thereby illustrating how prejudice divides the world. But, concludes the film, a divison line may be bent to form a circle to embrace all divisions—again a pictorial symbol for the theme of world cooperation.

The purpose of showing these films, aside from the excellent messages they contain, was to make the students aware of the collage techniques used to tell a story. Animated in Disney style but much more symbolic, the films used color (black for death, green for growth, red and purple for hate), line (X for conflict, S-shaped curves for beauty), and symbol (the actual eyes as the globe of the world, weapons for destruction, etc.) to portray vividly the sound track's message of world cooperation.

After the films there was a brief discussion designed to draw out this use of color, line, and organization as a conscious effort by the director to move his audience. From this discussion a project was suggested where each student might, through the use of similar symbols, tell a story of his own choosing.

On the day appointed by the classes for the beginning of this project, materials such as paints, clay, cardboards, construction paper, etc., were placed in the classroom. The only instructions given the students were these: "You may use these materials to tell a story, but be sure you can explain what it means should that be necessary."

Of all the materials available, perhaps the most important were approximately three hundred assorted magazines. From this source many of the boys cut illustrative pictures which they mounted in various ways on large pieces of cardboard. As might be expected, the more advanced students had more elaborate displays, emphasizing the picture with a color background or an unusual line pattern. Other students chose modernistic designs from the *Reader's Digest* (cubes, rectangles, etc.) and by the addition of color and careful, if conventional, symbolism (white cross for good, black wedge for sin) produced collages which revealed, as a matter of degree, their intuitive understanding of form.

A few students chose to work with clay. These boys were hampered somewhat by their medium, but such designs as the ship of life (an augury of Katherine Ann Porter's *Ship of Fools*, with color signifying the correspondence of various parts of the ship to life, that is, prow white for birth, stern black for death, with a kaleidoscope of colors between) and the wheel of life (colors again in sequence) were chosen.

All these student attempts at creativity produced a noticeable involvement, a commitment on the part of the students to fulfill an educational objective—for many, for the first time in their lives.[3] Over 75 percent of the class chose themes which illustrated some personal incident in their lives, while the rest of the class used contemporary events as their choice of topic. Once completed, the collages were mounted around the room with each author on stand-by alert to clarify or to extend the critical interpretations of his classmates. As a technique for approaching English, the collage in this first phase of the unit helped students to discover the role of forms and pattern in any design. But other chips in the mosaic that is English needed exploration, and such extensions of the collage technique are described below.

EXTENSIONS

Out of the explanations of their collages the boys gained insights into the environmental influences which cause authors to choose one word or symbol over another. For instance, sad or unfortunate emotional situations in many of the boys' lives were framed in blue. When questioned about the choice of this color, the boys stated that those particular incidents in their lives made them feel "blue." Similarly, red signaled danger, with stoplights, danger signs, fire engines, etc., entering their thought-processes. More involved, but in the same reasoning vein, linear symbols were examined. For example, in illustrating war, one boy, taking his black background, cut the periphery to produce a series of jagged edges, explaining that "war is a shattering experience." Other line formations were circles for life, post lintels for strength, crossroads and highways for crucial life decisions, ascending spirals for joy, descending spirals for despair, and crescents for happiness or sadness, depending upon the relation of the crescent points to the rest of the organization.

There was also some use made of texture (cotton for softness, iron spikes and nails for hardness, etc.) but perhaps the most important were the overall organization patterns. One could almost see the student's outlook on life by the way his collage was organized. Some students started at the top and worked to the bottom; others moved in a large semicircle; still others moved in an articulated sequence from bottom to top with smooth transition from one illustration to the next. Finally, the most maladjusted of the boys seemed to have little or no pattern at all, allowing their illustrations to meander.

One of the values offered by the collage technique in the teaching of English is that of diagnosing students' language problems. Students who consistently identify minor characters in a story as central to their collage illustration of the story imply by their choices an inability to identify hierarchial patterns used by many authors. Similarly, collages designed to reveal composition structures (comparison and contrast, analogy, development by detail) will also reveal student weaknesses in their choices of illustrative materials. Diagnoses such as these have a long research pedigree both in art and psychology and offer valuable insights into students' linguistic ills.[4]

But all this would avail nothing if the purpose of this project (to help students discover a gateway to *conventional* English) was not achieved. Apparently, the planned transfer took place, and textbook contents that formerly existed in a misty region of incomprehension began to stand out clearly and boldly in the minds of students. Let me illustrate.

APPLICATIONS

As mentioned earlier, "Language and Literature" was the focus of my first unit. And in that first disastrous week the textbook included under the heading "Adventure," S. V. Benet's "By the Waters of Babylon"[5] (a short story), Tennyson's "Gareth and Lynette," and Dickinson's "There Is No Frigate Like a Book" (poetry). Besides these materials I had acquired a taped performance of George R. Stewart's *Earth Abides*[6] (a novel) translated via tape to a dramatic form. Inasmuch as all these pieces of literature used the English language, my strategy was to have the students analyze the forms of the language within the context of the literary type and derive some insights about levels of usage and aphoristic messages. (As every English teacher knows, textbooks frequently badger us to have students draw a *moral* from the story; hence the concern for *message*.)

Knowing that the boys in the reform school would seldom sit through the reading of a novel, I was particularly smug about my cleverness in securing a novel in its dramatic form to startle the class into what I thought would be a high interest in the unit. *Earth Abides* poses the problem of survival for the few humans left after biological warfare has virtually eliminated man as a species. My hope was that students would identify themes such as man versus man or man versus nature, and be able to identify key points in the structure of the narrative which would help them to give it meaning.

Precollage, the boys concentrated on the material advantages of living in a depopulated world: free food, limitless access to fast cars, free gasoline, virtually anything a person could want for material comfort. When, at one point in the narrative, the protagonist is faced with the choice of taking either a gun or a hammer in his search for a new home in the depopulated wilderness, the students were unanimous in their disappointment in Isherwood's (the main character) choice of the hammer.

Postcollage, their reactions were the following. The hammer was used to build, so it might stand as a symbol for construction of a new world. The publication date (1949) might reflect the author's concern about an impending atomic war and its potential for the destruction of mankind. Insights about the price of progress seemed to be implied by the author's presentation of two types of scavengers, rats and men. Scavengerlike characters in Stewart's novel felt, as the students did, that "everything for free" meant an ideal existence. To illustrate the folly of their thinking Stewart used armies of rats motivated by the same "grasshopper" philosophy, and since the rats were parasitic and could not replace what they took, they soon eliminated themselves. After the collage, the author's use of rats as symbols and analogues of the human parasites led some students to the conclusion that survival is no accident; it has to be planned.

In spite of my captive audience, I should have known better than to try to approach poetry through the selections in a conventional textbook. But since the material was *there*, I fell into the same trap thousands of teachers do, namely, a belief that every selection in the textbook must be used. With the students' classical blocks to poetry, for example, "It's for girls; who needs it?" "We'll never use this junk," I still marvel that they cooperated with my attempt to teach "Gareth and Lynette" and "There Is No Frigate Like a Book." They considered both poems outdated and "stupid," but that was precollage.

Postcollage, re-examination of Tennyson's possible symbolism in his choice of the eagle and the golden palm led to suggestions that they might stand for everyone's search for glory, for a place in the sun. One way of achieving this recognition was the time-honored "battle" or war complicated by the problem of "momism," that is, the mother's refusal to recognize that the son was ready to leave the "nest." The mother-son conflict was deeply explored through the vicarious Gareth-mother, eagle-nest facades. Postcollage, too, the word *book* took on new meaning through exploration of Dickinson's perceptions; the idea of escape through books appealed to them, and they regarded her little *pome* as "cool."

Precollage, Benet's "By the Waters of Babylon" was most confusing to the students. Benet was a symbolist and in his short story introduced broken statuary with only parts of names to serve as cues for identifying the statues, for example, "ASHING" and "COLN" inscribed on two of the broken statues. Other enigmatic cues are the priests' chanting of "The Star Song" and identifying the river where the "place of the gods" was located as the "O-dis-sun." Of course, all these cues are found in the "burning place" which turned out to be New York City, generations after an atomic war.

Postcollage and as a direct result, I think, of students uses of symbols to tell a story, they were quick to recognize (W)"ashing"(ton) and (Lin)"coln" as the complete names on the commemorative statues; the "Star Song" as the "Star Spangled Banner"; and "O-dis-sun" as the Hudson River. Most important, they discussed the implications of superstition and diviniation as the end product of "gods" who ate knowledge too fast; then they tied Benet's story to Stewart's novel as a post-World War II literary theme. English skills such as identifying speaking voice, recognizing "how a story means," exploring vocabulary within the syntax of the idea presented, speculating about the possible themes from life which generate the story, and synthesizing all these problems into the organic work of art ("By the Waters of Babylon") helped them to deepen their understandings of all aspects of English as a discipline.

CONCLUSIONS

Collage techniques for teaching English to the disadvantaged are no panacea for students' linguistic and literary ills. Certainly, there are other media equally effective for breaking through the print curtain of the disadvantaged. But as one gateway to English skills, I am convinced that the collage technique can aid the teaching of English by: (1) giving each student a chance to design his own symbolic structure; (2) giving the teacher a diagnostic tool for assessing students' problems of organization, comprehension, transition, and meaning in their study of conventional English materials; (3) encouraging poorer students to relate stories in this medium and thereby gain knowledge of relationships between word choices (symbols) and their metaphorical impacts; and (4) helping students to clarify meanings in their study of conventional materials. A student cannot select an appropriate collage design for a grammatical or literary experience unless he thoroughly understands the sources of the ideas, be they textbook, paperback, or magazine. As Reismann pointed out in *The Culturally Deprived Child*,[7] such students are "thing oriented" and "game conscious." Both strategies for teaching English to disadvantaged youngsters are pivotal to the collage technique, which is why I recommend it as one gateway to English.

REFERENCES

1. William Nault, *Typical Course of Study, Grades 1 through 12* (Chicago: Field Enterprises, Inc., 1957), pp. 1-6.
2. Both films may be obtained from International Film Bureau, 6 North Michigan Avenue, Chicago 2, Illinois. Many film centers of the Anti Defamation League (ADL) also have rental copies available.
3. Richard Corbin, *Literacy, Literature and the Disadvantaged*, National Council of Teachers of English, Champaign, Illinois, 1964. Page 14 and *passim* make clear the excitement of this "discovery" among students who had previously accepted the judgment that they were too "dumb" to do anything but sit like vegetables in a classroom.
4. Cf. W. Phillips (ed.), *Art and Psychoanalysis*. (New York: Criterion

Books, 1957); W. R. Mueller, "Psychoanalyst and Poet: A Note," *Psychoanalysis* **5**, 55-56, 1957; R. Wilson, "The Poet and the Projective Test," *Journal of Aesthetics and Art Criticism* **16**, 319-327, 1958.

5. Robert Van Gelder (ed.), *The Stephen Vincent Benet Pocketbook* (New York: Pocket Books, Inc., 1946), pp. 178 ff.

6. George R. Stewart, *Earth Abides* (New York: Random House, 1949).

7. Frank Reismann, *The Culturally Deprived Child* (New York: Harper and Row, 1962).

Focus

The word "log" suggests many things from nautical records to Mark Hopkins. But the log which follows adds still another meaning to that versatile word. It is, in keeping with the theme of this book, the synthesis of the foregoing perceptions and, simultaneously, the application of cited references. It is a microcosm which answers the question, "What does all this material mean when translated to philosophy, teaching techniques, and subject matter for disadvantaged rural youth?"

Mrs. Helen Koch, author of the log, has taught English and Reading for some twenty years in rural, central Pennsylvania. She has been part of education's changing dimension—from high schools as foci for college bound to high schools as repository for all youth. She is respected and revered as a dedicated teacher by students who represent the educable range of the intelligence spectrum. Deeply concerned about providing useful learning situations for her disadvantaged students, Mrs. Koch immersed herself in institute work. Each film, each book, each media technique presented was examined critically, yet always with a searching purpose: how these devices might be used to improve her own classroom teaching. Mrs. Koch's log exemplifies sample principles and techniques around which one should organize an English or Reading course for disadvantaged youth, rural or urban.

Several unique qualities can be found in Mrs. Koch's perceptions. Bibliographies, for example, are rituals for most readers; but Mrs. Koch shows exactly which contents of bibliographical references are valuable for her work with the disadvantaged. Unique, too, is her derivation of overarching principles, based on institute experiences, for her working with her students. Finally, her organization of disparate elements into a unified perception predicated on a reasoned and observation-based rationale, makes her work a model for all who aspire to teach the disadvantaged. Her log is at once a pragmatic blueprint of documented principles for teaching the disadvantaged and a step-by-step description of the potential for change which the newer structures and processes gave to her hometown classes.

Media and the Disadvantaged

EDWARD R. FAGAN
HELEN M. KOCH

Contributors to this book described media as the bedrock for teaching the disadvantaged. They implied that media are best handled when two or more are presented within a single class period. Comprising the media are oral discourse, television, film, print, radio, and ancillary sensory stimuli, for example, photographs. Media impact on students in contemporary society is so pervasive that Patrick Hazard, Chairman of the English Department at Beaver College, urged teachers to consider media as the anticurriculum and to study it with the same intensity that physicists study antimatter in their field. Hazard's charge to the English teacher of the rural disadvantaged is based on the fact that disadvantaged students are not educated to cope with today's world even if they master the contents of the formal curriculum, because the anticurriculum, media, engages their interests and experience at a ratio of 7:1, where 1 represents the content of formal education.

The importance of media study—for everyone—is highlighted by Marshall McLuhan's controversial *Understanding Media*[1] which, among other things, points out that print as the status medium for communication is dying and that one positive factor in its demise is the tendency for man to rediscover and use his other senses. Because electronic media (television, radio) are so swift, the world has returned to a village society, that is, where rural verities such as face-to-face involvement prevail. And this immediate confrontation with reality is opposed to the increasingly archaic isolation imposed by the printed medium.

McLuhan's ideas are not new. In 1931 Edward Sapir, anthropologist-linguist, wrote prophetically in his article on "Communication" in the *Encyclopedia of the Social Sciences:*

The multiplication of far-reaching techniques of communication has two important results. In the first place it increases the sheer radius of

95

communication, so that for certain purposes the whole civilized world is made the psychological equivalent of a primitive tribe. In the second place, it lessens the importance of mere geographical contiguity. . . . This means, of course, a tendency to remap the world both sociologically and psychologically.[2]

Whereas Sapir's audience was limited and anything but a mass audience, Telstars and Early Birds attuned McLuhan's mass audience to his message. Movement from the print of Sapir's day to McLuhan's concept of instant involvement in world news "as it happens" was foreshadowed by artists at least twenty years ago. McLuhan cites the role of art in creating contemporary *involvement*, contemporary *heuristics*, and then goes on to show the impact of this sensory process on today's student.

> For several decades the artist has denied to the audience the mere consumer privilege of passive day-dreaming experience. He has urged the audience to participate in the creative process with all its arduous excitement.
> For many people this is confusing. But so is ordinary living. The child who from one to six years experiences an adult world in front of television is sent to school at six. He experiences there a carefully prepared child world for the first time in his life. This is very confusing. Most children may never recover from this traumatic experience which began only ten years ago. . . . Today our educational establishment has not come into rapport with our own technology, and there is little civil defense against media fall-out.[3]

Media, defined with such magnitude, encompass the entire field of English and the communication processes for teaching it. Within English as a field, teachers are urged to keep up with developments in linguistics, literature, composition, and a myriad of other new developments. Yet the rural English teacher, burdened with as many as 220 disadvantaged students, seven periods a day, is totally committed to his teaching task. He has all he can do to prepare his lessons, correct his compositions, and retain his sanity in an impossible situation. Clearly, some arrangement for freeing this teacher from his duties long enough to explore newer techniques and materials for teaching English is needed, and the 1964 extension of the National Defense Education Act (NDEA) to include institutes for teachers of disadvantaged youth provides such an opportunity.

ORIENTATION TO AN INSTITUTE

Using media as pivots for organizing institute experiences requires that institute participants understand the nature of an integrated program. One example of an integrated program which uses media as pivots takes three courses—Communication, Linguistics, and Reading—and combines their contents and teaching techniques so that an interlocking system is apparent. A characteristic of this interlocking system is the rotation of principles through the prism of media. The end product of this rotation is teacher understanding of each communication medium as it is defined and practiced by communication, linguistic, and reading specialists.

To illustrate the integration principle and to provide a background for the material which follows, picture a classroom within which are 30 participants selected for an NDEA institute for teachers of disadvantaged youth in rural areas. These participants are trying to absorb the contents of the above paragraph, to make some sense out of familiar words in an unfamiliar setting. Institute instructors, committed to the media-as-integration philosophy, make some of the following generalizations.

First, any classroom is a medium in the sense that there is a message exchange. Usually, teachers have a message which they try to communicate to the students. The students, in turn, attempt to fix the message clearly in mind. If students are confused about the message, they usually ask questions until the message transmitter, the teacher, by various techniques (repetition, illustration, rephrasing, etc.) clears up ambiguities about the message. Evaluation of message exchange—what techniques were used to encode and decode the message; what interference caused error, distortion, or ambiguity; what behavorial evidence showed that the message was understood—are all the subject matter of Communication.

Second, although the message process is fundamental to communication analysis, the medium (in this case the English language) is equally important for students' understanding. Consequently, the structure or patterns used in the message exchange, the pitch, stress, and intonation used to convey the pattern (if orally transmitted), and the key junctures as they increase or decrease message clarity are all principles of Linguistics. As a prelude to graphics (writing assignments), still other aspects of Linguistics (grammatical conventions and editing, for example) are part of media analysis in the classroom.

Finally, if print is part of the classroom message exchange, further complications are added to the encoding and decoding process. Organized around symbolic comprehension, print as it appears on the blackboard, in dittoed materials, or in textbooks requires some special techniques for message analysis. Though these specialized techniques are somewhat different from those used in Communication and Linguistics, the point is that Reading is a partial contributor to the whole classroom learning atmosphere. To treat Communication, Linguistics, and Reading as separate from the total learning environment is to ignore the fact that all three frequently occur simultaneously. Efficient learning is promoted when we take into account the total impact of all classroom media. If

such multiple evaluations are confusing (or border on the chaotic) remember McLuhan's dictum, "so is ordinary living." Life, particularly for
the rural disadvantaged, seldom operates in neatly packaged systems.

ORIENTATION TO THE LOG

Learning to think in simultaneous media is difficult. To help institute
participants develop guidelines for such thinking, institute instructors required all participants to keep *logs* of their daily institute experiences.
Hopefully, participants' reviews of such logs after their institute experiences would provide them with principles and guidelines for organizing
viable strategies for teaching English to students in their particular disadvantaged rural areas.

Using the truism "all teaching is based on a system," instructors pre-
scribed the system for keeping a log by pointing out that a log should
(1) state an idea, (2) explain why the idea was important, and (3) indicate
how the idea's importance might be translated into classroom behavior.
Helen Koch, an institute participant, organized her log around these three
prescriptions. What follows are excerpts from the Koch log which English
teachers of the disadvantaged may find useful. In reading the Koch log,
you are asked to identify as much as possible with Mrs. Koch. This identification implies that the reader, exposed to the ideas noted by Mrs. Koch,
has identified reactions to the new contents and techniques which were
the daily fare of institute participants. Such identification also implies
that the reader has something of the same background, experience, and
exposure to new ideas for teaching English that Mrs. Koch had. A gradu-
ate of a liberal arts program with a commitment to English as a discipline,
Mrs. Koch's teaching at one time focused on the college bound student
in most assigned English classes. But within the last decade she discovered
that 40 percent of the students in contemporary English classes are not
interested in academic English programs. Since these noncollege bound
students are there by law, some strategy for increasing their learning and
capturing their interest was necessary. Besides those strategies Mrs. Koch
devised for her classes, the insights she gathered via her institute experiences as reported below will provide media structures and simultaneous
processes for teaching the disadvantaged.

MEDIUM: ORAL DISCOURSE

Classroom discussions should be organized around the following
principles:

(1) Language is a symbol system which engages the physical, intellectual, and emotional behavior of the individual. Thought is usually per-

formed with language where thinking leads to decisions and choices which, in turn, lead to behavior.

(2) Decisions are made by weighing alternatives; alternatives are considered by the questions asked.

(3) Application of these principles for discussion within a classroom suggests that some alternative to classroom questioning as it now exists is necessary because (a) in school, students constantly deal with somebody else's questions; (b) what we do as teachers is based on what questions we ask ourselves; and (c) questions must be structured for the answer desired.

As English teachers, the foregoing suggest that we cue students to language as the center for human learning and that we raise questions about language as a system. Point out, for example, that football, basketball, and card players use a system. Get students to describe other examples of systems. Ask students what language does for them. Help them to see language as a system in operation by asking:

(1) How does the language you use with your parents differ from the language you use with your friends?

(2) How does your language tell things about you?

(3) What short words may have more power than long words (*fire* versus *conflagration*)?

(4) What changes have you noticed in language since our space program began?

(5) Why don't I always understand you, and you me?

(6) How old is our language?

(7) What would we need to have a universal language?

The students' answers to these questions may be startling, humorous, or conservative, but they are not *wrong* in the usual sense of that word. Such questions might get at some history of language and possibly its uses—a form of usage study.

As to the exploration of language content or Communication, we as teachers might organize our oral discourse around applications of Ashley Montagu's *Education and Human Relations* quote, "Disadvantaged youth need in this stage of training in human relations, survival, and the feeling of getting by. Language is the key to this."

Classroom principles implicit in Montagu's statement might be as follows:

(1) We are all trying to survive and our biggest problem is to make sense, to sort out, to discover possibilities of what we are going to do.

(2) We never get meaning from anything; we give meaning to something.

(3) Learning takes place by someone asking a question that has not been asked before.

Application of these principles might include asking students: "What makes an expert?" (the kind of question he asks); "What makes a good doctor?" (his ability to ask his patient the right question); "How do judgments stop thought?" (judgments stop thinking by a person's response to the classification of judgment, for example, nigger, jew).

Since most of the official school language is threatening—statements of penalty—students' questions and their acceptance by the teacher are vital. Creative children ask questions that others do not ask.

The objective of all communication, in or out of the classroom, is agreement. Whether literature, language, or composition is involved, the objective of the message transmission is understanding and agreement. If we as teachers can structure the questions properly, we will get more controlled behavior and response. Behavior is directly related to the way that we handle language.

Principles about the medium of oral discussion in teaching English to the disadvantaged imply the following strategies:

(1) careful teacher selection of content for classroom discussion based on a variety of media, for instance, tapes, records, films, books, etc.;

(2) systematic questioning designed to help students give meaning to the material being considered;

(3) organizing all questions so that principles of Communication, Linguistics, and Reading are considered within the exploration of all materials used in English classrooms.

MEDIUM: TELEVISION

If people had to decide upon only one medium, television would probably be their choice. It is the most exciting, power absorbing, and stimulating medium for the average citizen. Because of its impact we cannot afford to be illiterate in television evaluation, yet most of our schools are oriented toward print in spite of the fact that most of the reading in the nation is done by less than 10 percent of the population. Television appeals to students via vicarious experience, humor, aesthetics, self-rating programs, and human contact against loneliness. Television beams its programs to specific audiences, but few English classes study audience analysis. Lack of viewers' critical facilities led to unflattering definitions of television as "chewing gum for the eyes" and an "idiot bar."

Television is an art form and art forms tend to shape us. We construct a building and the building shapes us; we invent a language and the language shapes our thinking; we invent print and print shapes us.

At present we are a print-oriented people who nevertheless avoid print except in school. Students are as illiterate toward books as they are toward other media, yet other media can serve to bridge the literacy gap, and television is a major medium for accomplishing this. While newspaper reading is something of a ritual and magazine reading is a form of browsing, television requires involvement; it is sight, plus sound, plus emotion. As a medium it is not just the pipeline through which reality is pumped; it actually shapes the reality we perceive.

Applying these ideas to the classroom, we recall that one reason for classifying our rural English students as disadvantaged is that they know very little. Since one learns only from something one knows, it is not surprising that disadvantaged students learn little in a print-oriented system. Television is one medium for adding to what the disadvantaged student should know. Ways of doing this might include:

(1) teaching the Laswell formula, that is, "who," "said what," "to whom," "in what media," "with what effect," as an evaluative device for television programs;

(2) compiling a list of video tapes and kinescopes made available free of charge by various companies which relate to English teaching, for example, *The Alphabet Conspiracy* (Bell Telephone Company), *Minerva's Children* (Armstrong Cork Company), and *Sixteen in Webster Groves* (Columbia Broadcasting System);

(3) assigning projects which draw heavily on commercial or educational television viewing, for example, a graph of students' viewing habits, a filmstrip illustration of the persuasive techniques used by commercials, a written report of some program related to English, for instance, Ambrose Bierce's *Incident at Owl Creek Bridge* as dramatized on "Twilight Zone";

(4) organizing program reports for the local area in the style of *TV Guide;*

(5) identifying the questioning technique used on quiz shows and the like to discover techniques for asking questions.

From this use of television as a medium should come an increase in the students' ability to sort out alternatives in problem situations. In all cases the processes used are important to the discovery of meaning.

MEDIUM: FILMS

Editing, a skill we seldom teach in English (we talk about "teaching" writing and composition) is best exemplified in television and films. Using the film *Shooting and Editing of Gunsmoke,*[4] we can present a subject high in national television ratings and a process badly needed in all aspects of English teaching. The film shows twenty minutes of scenes from "Gun-smoke" which were then edited by three directors. After editing, the scenes which appeared on the television screens took about six to ten seconds. Students should be asked to compare this editing function with their writing and to devise some ideas about the differences between writing and editing.

One possible transition between the film and writing might be students' uses of their own still photography or moving pictures. Many homes have old photographs lying around. The student assignment would be to arrange a series of these photographs into a story or essay. In reporting on their projects, students should be able to describe the basis for their editorial work, that is, why this picture was included and another eliminated, why this picture was used before instead of after a given pictorial sequence. From such creative experiences students should evolve the following principles:

(1) Any given sequence of pictures depends upon the author's purpose.

(2) Organization of an artistic experience requires interpretation as well as assessment of values.

(3) Sensitivity to local surroundings is a function of involvement with an artistic experience.

It is not likely that disadvantaged students in rural areas will describe their picture-story experience in the foregoing terms, but language sophistication aside, they should come close to the ideas listed. As teachers we would discover that children writing about pictures they have taken develop a sophistication that is surprising.

An experience which might summarize the picture-story assignment and reinforce the writing-editing aspects of film might be provided by their viewing *A Divided World*. There is no sound to this film. It begins with a bubble in a pool of water, then shifts to a quiet wood. Within the wood the camera closeup shows a weasel eating a dead bird. The camera then focuses on a rabbit under the surveillance of a coyote; the coyote attacks and kills the rabbit, but an owl drives off the coyote and devours the rabbit. The scene then shifts from the woods to a plowed field and a solitary house against the night sky. And there it ends. For every ten feet of this firm shot, only one foot appeared on the screen. The editing here was at the ratio of 9:1.

Students after viewing this silent film should be able to notice such techniques as camera shifts and their effects; they should develop insights about "silent language," the theme of Robert Hall's book, *The Silent Language*. All animals in the film (perhaps with the exception of man) knew the code, the language of nature. Who would survive, and why, was known by the participants and by the film's director, Arne Sucksdorff.

Two films that might be used as a comparison and contrast technique for sensitizing students to the changes in the grammar of film might be *The Cry of the Children* and *Eye of the Beholder*. The first film was shot about sixty years ago with a stationary camera; all shots are from the same angle; there is no panning and no closeups; characters are stereotypes, and the film "preaches" the lesson that unions are the only recourse for the elimination of child labor. The other more recent film implies that language is used by human beings for human purposes. The film's main character is seen by various people as what they judge him to be: a good son, a hood, crazy, a murderer. Tacitly, this film illustrates the point of oral discourse as a medium when it implies judgments stop thinking. Both films would prove a useful beginning for writing assignments.

Applying the ideas of film as a medium for teaching English to the disadvantaged in rural areas might include the following principles:

(1) When a child starts to school he is a question mark; when he comes out he is a period. One of the ways to avoid such genocide is to widen students' experience, to pique students' curiosity via the film medium.

(2) Editing, an English skill badly needed but seldom taught, can be effectively illustrated via the film medium; it should have direct application to students' composition and writing skills.

(3) Frequent uses of film are needed in disadvantaged classrooms so that (a) students can widen their horizons about the grammar of an artistic medium, and (b) students can develop criteria for judging the worth of films.

(4) Films should be used as much as possible with the every English unit because of their increasing use as an instructional tool by such enterprises as 8 mm film projects, the *Commission on English*, the *Encyclopedia Britannica Films*, etc., and as edited ways for studying various aspects of English as a discipline.[5]

MEDIUM: PRINT

Print includes newspapers, magazines, catalogs, pamphlets, brochures, and maps as well as textbooks and anthologies. In common, all forms of print use a symbol system that must be learned for student comprehension. Where disadvantaged students are concerned, particularly at the junior high school level, prerequisites to understanding print are often assumed to be present in students' backgrounds or simply in need of review. Two of these prerequisites are listening and observing as distinguished from hearing and seeing.

One strategem for sharpening prerequisites for the study of print would be to use the format of the old "Twenty Questions" show or any other TV program that uses skillful questioning as a technique. Rules for the questions (just as rules for print) must be understood by the students. These rules might consist of the following:

(1) Answers must be "yes" or "no," so questions must be framed to be answered in that way. So long as a "yes" answer is given, the questioner may continue; as soon as a "no" answer is given, the questioning moves to another student.

(2) Keep track of what you know.

(3) Avoid wild guesses. The process involves putting together bits of information.

(4) Vary the direction of the question according to some system.

(5) Structure the questions according to characteristics, location, and range of the unknowns involved.

(6) Check assumptions, that is, make sure the question will advance what already is known.

(7) Too many "no" answers imply a wrong direction and suggest a shift in assumptions.

After developing some skill with this game, students should be able to draw generalizations from it which will be helpful for their involvement with print. Examples of such generalizations might be as follows: recognizing useful questions and the reasons for their being classified as useful; sorting information obtained into priorities according to some system; generating insights about how to confront a problem, how to ask a question.

Other strategies based on students' observational skills might consist of film strips, cartoons, or stick drawings made by the teacher which focus on one or more details. For example, announcing that a ball over the right field fence usually means a left-handed batter, then flashing a group of ball players in batting stance on a screen (one player an obvious left-hander) for one or two seconds, blocking the screen off and asking for the identification of the left-handed batter in the group by his position from the left side of the screen or from the numeral on his shirt. A whole series of exercises such as this would improve observation and, coincidentally, skill in left-to-right eye movements.

Disadvantaged students are obviously involved in this gamemanship (a recommended technique for work with the disadvantaged according to Frank Riessman in the *Culturally Deprived Child*). Other media besides print (as pointed out earlier) help to provide prerequisites to print as a medium. Telling stories through still photographs or film, or captioning pictures clipped from magazines are other means of warming students to the printed medium. These exercises direct the students' attention toward details within a context and toward the rules which set the limits for print experiences. Both these foci are critical for understanding print but, more important, they lay a foundation for student writing.

Reading, according to most research studies, is one of the best means for improving students' writing.[6] At least one college course in Freshman Composition is built upon reading,[7] and the point made by such research about writing is that, as Paul Roberts put it, there is nothing more useless in English today than the 500 word theme. To write, students must have stimulating ideas; one source of stimulating ideas is printed material. Roma Gans[8] suggested that the seductions of advertising, the one-sided point of view of many media, and the unrealistic content of literature are all subjects which whet students' critical skills in media analysis.

Relationships between reading and writing are implicit in Deborah Elkins' study[9] of the effects of common content on seventh graders' language arts skills. Organized around the theme "We Learn from Our Families," some of the findings about common content as a language arts strategem were as follows.

(1) Concepts chosen for common themes should be important to students and society.

(2) Teachers should not try to teach all children the same thing at the same time.

(3) All writing topics must be close to students' experiences and concrete enough so that the assignments are real to them.

(4) Oral reading and evaluation of students' listening skills should be continual so that adaptations in teaching techniques can reinforce areas revealed as weak via oral-aural feedback.

(5) Heuristics, student discovery, is necessary to maintain student excitement about the media contents studied.

Another study which supports the Elkins findings and reveals again the interdisciplinary nature of English is that of Maurine Hardin, which details the process of the common theme "The Proper Study of Mankind Is Man." In this case the class, divided into groups, was confronted with six novels. Each group was asked to select one of the six for detailed study, told to develop criteria in support of the novel selected, and asked to suggest a class theme for the unit. Notice that student involvement was immediate; decisions and responsibilities for their actions were implicit in their sorting processes. Students developed a series of questions to be answered in the study of the novel selected (compare with questioning techniques). Student groups were assigned by students to handle categories of questions relating to character, theme, and so on. Subgroups were assigned the task of complementing ideas from the novels with selections from poetry and drama. Still other subgroups were given the opportunity to write and develop a dramatic presentation. This presentation brought the groups back into a full scale class project again and, after it had been taped, the tape was used as one criterion for evaluating the entire project. In this evaluation, as they did in every step of the project, students took part.

While Miss Hardin's project is neither new nor startling, it demonstrates again the fact that student involvement—particularly the involvement of disadvantaged students—in such projects increases the students' learning and interest via a multiple media strategem planned by the teacher.

CONCLUSION

Only the media dimensions of Mrs. Koch's log are excerpted for the reader's judgment in the foregoing material. In their original state, the statements were cryptic phrases or sentences usually supported by equally cryptic examples. The elaboration and extensions of Mrs. Koch's viewpoints attempted to show the meanings she gave to the contents of her courses in Communication, Linguistics, and Reading. Her meanings were primarily statements of principles and concepts instead of lists of materials and the "how to's" about reading a newspaper or classifying propaganda techniques in films. Valuable as such details are (and references for them can be found in the Bibliography), the authors of this book feel that such lists and "how to's" are useless unless we as teachers have clearly in mind principles, concepts, and philosophies which determine the selection of content and the methods for teaching English to disadvantaged students in rural schools. Once the nature of these trigger systems is understood, the materials and "how to's" can be gathered anywhere, preferably from the local area, but from recommended lists if the trigger systems' eclectic dictates their usefulness.

Another virtue of Mrs. Koch's log is its evidence of the fact that the meaning of interdisciplinary study was understood and applied. The linear nature of print and its circumscribed appeal to sight is illustrated throughout this book, yet Mrs. Koch's grasp of the impact of media other than print for helping disadvantaged students to move into a print-oriented school situation is well illustrated.

EPILOGUE

During the academic year (September 1965 to June 1966) Mrs. Koch tried some of the ideas described in the foregoing log. Her August 1966 report can be summarized as follows.

(1) She was assigned to teach "remedial reading" to the seventh and eighth grades. All teachers sent to her classes students whom they identi-

fied as needing help in reading. Students attended her classes twice a week on a voluntary basis, and by the end of the year she had an enrollment of 300 students.

(2) Mrs. Koch's first application of the meanings she gave to institute principles was to inform all students that their work in her classes was "skill building"; consequently, "remedial reading" should not be used to describe the classes. Mrs. Koch hoped that this semantic difference would remove the onus of "dumb" classes attached traditionally to the remedial reading label.

(3) Newspaper reading was the first class unit, and students were asked to read the newspaper to keep informed not only in English but also in science and social studies.

(4) Students in their newspaper reading began to question how much accurate information was contained in advertising. Advertising, as presented via radio and television, was the next area for student investigation, and, based on student discussion, verification, and comparison, guidelines for evaluating the accuracy not only of advertising but also of news reporting in all media were developed.

(5) Extensions of the guidelines developed by the students to evaluate films from the Film Library of Indiana University in Pennsylvania were followed by heated discussions about the function of editing and the responsibilities of film editors. Students enjoyed the opportunities to raise questions about such matters in class.

(6) Some of the problems of editing information to fit a rigid time schedule led students to wonder about the technical difficulties which went into such editing. By presenting within specified time blocks (for example, a ten minute program) various word games, pattern drills, and dramatic skits via the tape recorder, students developed an ear for linguistic detail and an understanding of an editor's problems. (Mrs. Koch notes, "The tape recorder did more to improve oral reading and speaking than any other technique used.")

(7) Editing to fit predetermined structures within a fixed time and, simultaneously, to provide for some classroom creativity, students made good use of the collage as a "composition" technique on such subjects as "Recreation," "Hobbies," and "What Makes a Happy Kid."

At this point in the Epilogue, it seems fitting to let Mrs. Koch close her report in her own words.

> The "Twenty Questions" game was a favorite, and its popularity spread to other classes. After a few games, many of the students realized that they could get more information from asking good questions than from merely guessing. The science teacher told me there was a marked improvement in the kind of questions asked in science class after this game had been used. The students asked to play it in

science class. Any time we had a few spare minutes in class, someone always suggested "Twenty Questions."

Throughout the year, the classes were informal and lively. I think the students felt there was freedom in the class and this was different from the pressure exerted in other classes. I do not mean that all students were totally enthusiastic about the course, but not one of the 300 complained about the course or asked to be removed from it.[10]

REFERENCES

1. Marshall McLuhan, *Understanding Media* (New York: McGraw-Hill, 1964).

2. Quoted in Lennox Grey, *What Communication Means Today* (Champaign, Illinois: National Council of Teachers of English, 1944), p. 30.

3. Marshall McLuhan, "Grammars for the Newer Media," *Communication in General Education*, Frances Shoemaker and Louis Forsdale (eds.), (Dubuque, Iowa: William C. Brown Company, 1960), p. 24.

4. Available from Audio-Visual Services Division of The Pennsylvania State University.

5. John M. Culkin, "Mass Media Study in the Schools," *National Catholic Educational Association (NCEA) Bulletin*, **59**, 12-28, February 1963.

6. W. H. Evans, "Composition, Reading, and the Conant Report," *High School Journal*, **46**, 268-278, May 1963.

7. S. Leonard Rubinstein, "Composition: Collision with Literature," *College English*, **27**, 273-277, January 1966.

8. Roma Gans, "Critical Reading for the Sixties," *Improving Reading Instruction* (University Park, Pennsylvania: The Pennsylvania State University Press, 1963), pp. 1-6.

9. Deborah Elkins, *Reading Improvement in the Junior High School* (New York: Bureau of Publications, Teachers College, Columbia University, 1963).

10. Helen Koch (personal letter), August 14, 1966.

A FRAME OF REFERENCE AND PROCEDURE TO FACILITATE CATEGORIZATION OF TEACHERS' STATEMENTS

Each statement made by the teacher contains *one* of two dominant kinds of intent. These are either (1) intent to sustain the teacher and his behavior (teacher-centered statements) or (2) intent to sustain the learner and his behavior (learner-centered statements and issue-centered statements are included here). By analysis of both the *context* and the *content* of a teacher's statement it may be possible to determine whether the dominant intent of a statement is to sustain the teacher or the learner. Once the dominant intent of the statement has been ascertained, one can proceed to determine the technique by which the support is conveyed.

(1) If the statement is intended primarily to *sustain the teacher,* one or possibly a combination of the two following techniques may be used:

(a) reproof of the learner (Category 6); (b) directing or advising the learner (Category 5). Frequently the intent of the statement is to sustain the teacher yet neither of the above techniques is used. In that event the statement is simply a self-supportive remark which defends the teacher or evidences perseveration in support of the teacher's position or ideas (Category 7).

(2) If the intent of a statement is to *sustain the learner,* then one or possibly a combination of the two following techniques may be used:

(a) clarification and acceptance of the learner's feelings or ideas (Category 2);

(b) problem structuring statements (Category 3).

Frequently the intent of a statement is to sustain the learner yet neither of the above techniques is used. In that event the statement is simply one that reassures, commends, agrees with, or otherwise sustains the learner (Category 1).

Infrequently a statement by the teacher may have no dominant intent to sustain either the teacher or the learner. If the statement represents neither of the techniques in the two intent areas nor gives evidence of being one of the more general kinds of supporting statements, then the statement can be considered to have no intent to support and should be placed in Category 4.

Recourse to the learner's statement or behavior before and after a teacher's response, particularly when one encounters a statement in which the intent is difficult to ascertain, is sometimes helpful in categorizing the teacher's statements.

REFERENCES

John Withall. "The Development of a Technique for the Measurement of Social-Emotional Climate in Classrooms," *Journal of Experimental Education*, Vol. XVIII, No. 3, March 1949.

John Withall. *Impact on Learners of Climate Created by the Teacher* (film), Bureau of Audio-Visual Instruction, University of Wisconsin, Madison, Wisconsin, 1963.

appendix **B**

SOCIAL EMOTIONAL CLIMATE INDEX: CRITERIA FOR CATEGORIES OF TEACHERS' STATEMENTS

CATEGORY 1. LEARNER-SUPPORTIVE STATEMENTS OR QUESTIONS

These are the teacher's statements or questions that express agreement with the ideas, actions, or opinions of the learner, or that commend or reassure the learner. Agreement is frequently expressed by a monosyllabic response such as "Yes," "Right," "Uhuh," and the like. Commendation or reassurance may be stated in terms of (1) criteria or goals accepted by the class, or (2) the private goals and subjective criteria of the teacher. The dominant intent of these statements or questions is to *praise, encourage,* or *bolster the learner.*

Examples of statements or questions in Category 1 are: "That's fine, Bill, you've helped the class a lot." "Good for you, Joan!" "Aren't you the one who brought in these excellent illustrations, Sam?" "How do you think up so many interesting comments?"

CATEGORY 2. ACCEPTANT OR CLARIFYING STATEMENTS OR QUESTIONS

These are statements or questions of the teacher which either (1) accept, that is, evidence considerable understanding by the teacher of, or (2) clarify, that is, restate clearly and succinctly in the teacher's words the ideational or the feeling content of the learner's statement. The *dominant intent* of these responses by the teacher is to *help the learner* to gain insight into his problem, that is, define his *real* problem and its solution in more operational terms and to convey the depth of the teacher's comprehension of the learner's problem and solution.

Examples of statements or questions in Category 2 are: "As you said, it's very complicated." "I know just how you feel. I get frustrated too when I work hard and long and get nowhere." "If I understand you rightly, we should take the square root, sum the means, and finally divide by 100 to find the proportion." "As I get it, you'll analyze the historical facts from McCauley's history, add the material that you got from Waverley's chapters, and wind up with your concluding paragraph."

CATEGORY 3. PROBLEM-STRUCTURING STATEMENTS OR QUESTIONS

Problem-structuring responses by the teacher offer facts, ideas, or opinions to the learner about phenomena or procedures in a nonthreatening and objective manner. These responses contain no element of advising or recommending the adoption of certain ideas or procedures. Problem-structuring responses are frequently posed as questions which seek further information from the learner about the problem confronting him; or they may be statements which offer information to the learner about his problem. The learner is free to accept or to reject in part or in entirety the facts or opinions that are presented to him. Problem-structuring responses may be questions which the teacher asks (1) to further increase her own understanding of what the learner has said, or (2) to increase the precision of the learner's statement of the problem. Problem-structuring responses are problem-centered rather than either teacher- or learner-centered; nevertheless, they do tend to sustain the learner by facilitating his problem-solving activities.

Examples of statements or questions in Category 3 are: "What is the distance of the moon from the earth?" "πr^2 is the formula for finding the area of a circle." "Do a feather and a lump of lead fall at the same speed in a vacuum?" "Sound travels at approximately 700 miles per hour in the air."

CATEGORY 4. NEUTRAL STATEMENTS EVIDENCING
NO SUPPORTIVE INTENT

These statements are neither teacher sustaining, nor learner sustaining, nor problem-centered. They constitute a small percentage of the total responses of the teacher. These responses include statements in which the teacher (1) questions herself aloud, (2) repeats verbatim a statement that the learner has just made, (3) uses a polite formality, and so on. Statements having to do with administrative procedure (the room in which the class will meet, the hour at which a conference will occur: especially after consensus has been achieved) fall into this category.

Examples of statements or questions in Category 4 are: "We were looking at page 212 yesterday." "I'm sorry, I didn't quite catch what you said." "May I help?" "Let's meet at noon tomorrow." "Please excuse my clumsiness."

CATEGORY 5. DIRECTIVE STATEMENTS OR QUESTIONS

These are a teacher's statements or questions which advise the learner regarding a course of action or his future behavior and which narrowly limit his choice or offer no choice. These statements recommend to the learner the facts or procedures that the teacher proffers him. They convey the impression to the learner that the teacher expects and hopes that he will follow her prompting and that she will approve if he does. The *intent* of these responses is to have the learner accept the teacher's point of view and pursue a course of action that she advocates.

Examples of statements or questions in Category 5 are: "That's to be in by the twelfth without fail." "Why not do it the way I recommended in the first place?" "That's to be completed before you leave." "I'd appreciate your doing it in accordance with the proposed outline."

CATEGORY 6. REPROVING, DISAPPROVING, OR DISPARAGING STATEMENTS OR QUESTIONS

By means of these statements a teacher may express complete or partial disapproval of the ideas, behavior, and, to her, personality weaknesses of the learner. The teacher's internalized societal values largely enter into these responses. By means of these statements some teachers believe that they are fulfilling their responsibility of inculcating in young people society's standards of acceptable and desirable behavior and achievement. The *intent* of these statements is:

(1) to represent to the learner societal values as the teacher sees them,

(2) to admonish the learner for unacceptable behavior and to deter him from repeating it in the future, or

(3) to impress on the learner the fact that he has not met the criteria for successful achievement which the teacher holds.

Examples of statements or questions in Category 6 are: "You people are always griping about something." "If you had listened you would have heard." "Why don't you buckle down and get to work for a change?" "That's a stupid question." "You mean to say that's all you did?" "Considering you did it, that's not bad."

CATEGORY 7. TEACHER-SUPPORTIVE STATEMENTS OR QUESTIONS

These are statements or questions in which the teacher refers to herself and expresses a defensive attitude, or refers to her present or past interests, activities, or possessions with the purpose of reassuring herself and of confirming her position or her ideas in the eyes of those around her. The *dominant intent* of the teacher's responses in this case is to *assert*, to *defend*, or to *justify* herself. Statements in which the teacher perseverates on an idea, a belief, or a suggestion would fall into this category. By perseveration is meant a persisting in, a reiteration of, and a rigid advocacy of an idea or opinion by the teacher despite additional data being presented to her which calls for re-examination of the original idea or opinion.

Examples of statements or questions in Category 7 are: "You know as well as I that I don't make unreasonable demands." "Aren't my questions usually clear and concise though?" "I extended myself especially to suit your convenience."

BIBLIOGRAPHY

BOOKS

AGEE, JAMES. *Let Us Now Praise Famous Men.* Boston: Houghton-Mifflin Co., 1960.

ALLEN, GEORGE N. *Undercover Teacher.* Garden City, New York: Doubleday and Co., Inc., 1960.

ASHTON-WARNER, SYLVIA. *Teacher.* New York: Simon and Schuster, 1963.

ASSOCIATION FOR SUPERVISION AND CURRICULUM DEVELOPMENT. *Perceiving, Behaving, Becoming: A New Focus for Education.* Washington, D.C.: The Association, 1962.

BALCER, CHARLES L., and HUGH F. SEABURY. *Teaching Speech in Today's Secondary Schools.* New York: Holt, Rinheart, and Winston, Inc., 1965.

BETTELHEIM, BRUNO. *Love Is Not Enough.* Glencoe, Ill.: Free Press, 1950.

BLOOM, BENJAMIN S., ALLISON DAVIS, and ROBERT HESS. *Compensatory Education for Cultural Deprivation.* New York: Holt, Rinehart, and Winston, Inc., 1965.

BRINK, WILLIAM. *The Negro Revolution in America.* New York: Simon and Schuster, Inc., 1963.

BROWN, B. FRANK. *The Non-Graded High School.* Englewood Cliffs, N.J.: Prentice-Hall, Inc., 1964.

———. *The Appropriate Placement School.* Englewood Cliffs, N.J.: Parker Publications, 1966.

CLARK, KENNETH B. *Dark Ghetto.* New York: Harper and Row, 1965.

CLELAND, DONALD L. (ed.). *Reading in the Content Areas.* University of Pittsburgh, Report of the Fifteenth Annual Conference and Course on Reading, 1959.

CROSBY, MURIEL (ed.). *Reading Ladders for Human Relations,* 4th ed. Washington, D.C.: American Council on Education, 1963.

CROW, LESTER D., WALTER I. MURRAY, and HUGH M. SMYTHE. *Educating the Culturally Disadvantaged Child.* New York: David McKay Co., Inc., 1966.

DAVIS, ALLISON. *Social-Class Influences upon Learning.* Cambridge, Mass.: Harvard University Press, 1950.

DURKIN, DOLORES. *Phonics and the Teaching of Reading.* New York: Bureau of Publications, Teachers College, Columbia University, 1965.

EDUCATIONAL POLICIES COMMISSION. *Mass Communication and Education.* Washington, D.C.: NEA, 1958.

115

ELKINS, DEBORAH. *Reading Improvement in the Junior High School*. New York: Bureau of Publications, Teachers College, Columbia University, 1963.

FERNALD, GRACE. *Remedial Techniques in Basic School Subjects*. New York: McGraw-Hill Book Company, 1943.

FINOCCHIARO, MARY. *Teaching English as a Second Language in Elementary and Secondary Schools*. New York: Harper and Row, 1958.

FRIEDENBERG, EDGAR Z. *The Vanishing Adolescent*. New York: Dell Publishing Co., Inc., 1959.

FRIES, CHARLES C. *Linguistics and Reading*. New York: Holt, Rinehart, and Winston, Inc., 1963.

FROMM, ERICH. *The Art of Loving*. New York: Harper and Row, 1956.

FROST, JOE L., and GLENN R. HAWKES. *The Disadvantaged Child: Issues and Innovations*. Boston: Houghton-Mifflin Co., 1966.

GANS, ROMA. *Guilding Children's Reading Through Experiences*. New York: Bureau of Publications, Teachers College, Columbia University, 1962.

GOLDEN, RUTH. *Improving Patterns of Language Usage*. Detroit: Wayne State University Press, 1960.

GOODE, W. *The Family*. Englewood Cliffs, N.J.: Prentice-Hall, Inc., 1964.

GOODMAN, PAUL. *Growing Up Absurd*. New York: Random House, 1956.

HARRINGTON, M. *The Other America*. New York: The Macmillan Co., 1964.

HEILMAN, ARTHUR (ed.). *Improving Reading Instruction*. University Park, Pa.: The Pennsylvania State University, 1964. Also *Education for Tomorrow: Reading*. University Park, Pa.: The Pennsylvania State University, 1965.

HERSEY, JOHN. *The Child Buyer*. New York: Alfred Knopf, 1950.

HICKERSON, NATHANIEL. *Education for Alienation*. Englewood Cliffs, N.J.: Prentice-Hall, Inc., 1966 (paperback).

HOLBROOK, DAVID. *English for the Rejected*. New York: Cambridge University Press, 1964.

HOLT, JOHN. *How Children Fail*. New York: Pitman Publishing Co., 1964.

JEWETT, ARNO, JOSEPH MERSAND, and DORIS GUNDERSON. *Improving English Skills of Culturally Different Youth*, Office of Education Bulletin No. 5. Washington, D.C.: U.S. Department of Health, Education, and Welfare, 1964.

KING, MARTIN L. *Why We Can't Wait*. New York: Harper and Row, 1964.

Listening Aids Through the Grades. New York: Bureau of Publications, Teachers College, Columbia University, 1959.

MASSEY, WILL. J., and VIRGINIA D. MOORE. *Helping High School Students to Read Better*. New York: Holt, Rinehart, and Winston, Inc., 1965.

NOAR, GERTRUDE. *Teaching and Learning the Democratic Way*. Englewood Cliffs, N.J.: Prentice-Hall, Inc., 1963.

PASSOW, A. HARRY (ed.). *Education in Depressed Areas*. New York: Bureau of Publications, Teachers College, Columbia University, 1963.

REMMERS, H. H., and D. H. RADLER. *The American Teenager*. New York: The Bobbs-Merrill Co., Inc., 1957.

RIESSMAN, FRANK. *The Culturally Deprived Child*. New York: Harper and Row, 1962.

ROGERS, CARL. *On Becoming a Person.* Boston: Houghton-Mifflin Co., 1961.
SEXTON, PATRICIA. *Education and Income.* New York: The Viking Press, 1961.
TROW, WILLIAM C. *Teacher and Technology: New Designs for Learning.* New York: Appleton-Century-Crofts, 1963.

ARTICLES AND JOURNALS

ALSTON, F. C., and R. O. WILLIAMS. "Johnny Doesn't—Didn't Hear," *Journal of Negro Education,* 35 (Spring 1964), pp. 197-201.
ARNEZ, N. L. "A Study of Attitudes of Negro Teachers and Pupils Toward School," *Journal of Negro Education,* 32 (Summer 1963), pp. 289-293.
Audio Visual Instruction, 10, No. 4 (April 1965).
AYER, G. E. "Notes on My Native Sons—Education in Harlem," *Freedomways,* 3 (Summer 1963), pp. 375-383.
BETTLEHEIM, BRUNO. "Teaching the Disadvantaged," *NEA Journal,* 54 (September 1965), pp. 8-12.
BROWN, HARRIETT B., and ELINOR D. SINETTE. "The School Library Program for Children in a Depressed Area," *ALA Bulletin,* 58 (July-August 1964), pp. 643-647.
Childhood Education, 39 (May 1963). Association for Childhood Education, Washington, D.C. Contains articles such as "Children in Crowded Areas," "Seeds of Drop-Outs," "All-Day Neighborhood School Programs," "After School Program."
CONANT, J. B. "New Conant Report: Excerpts," *Senior Scholastic* (October 18, 1962).
DANIEL, W. G. "Editorial Comment: Educational Planning for Socially Disadvantaged," *Journal of Negro Education,* 33 (Summer 1964), pp. 203-209.
DAVIDSON, HELEN, and GERHARD LANG. "Children's Perceptions of Their Teachers' Feelings Toward Them Related to Self-Perception, School Achievement, and Behavior," *Journal of Experimental Education* (December 1960), pp. 107-118.
DELLA-DORA, DELMO. "The Culturally Disadvantaged," *Exceptional Child,* 29 (January 1963), p. 226.
EDUCATIONAL POLICIES COMMISSION OF THE NEA. "Education and the Disadvantaged American," *NEA Journal,* 10 (April 1962).
EDWARDS, FRANKLIN. "Marriages and Family Life," *Journal of Negro Education,* 33 (Fall 1963), pp. 451-465.
EDWARDS, THOMAS. "The Language Experience Attack on Cultural Deprivation," *The Reading Teacher,* 18 (April 1965).
FOSTER, JOY L. "Tenth Grade English for Slow Learners," *Clearing House,* 34 (November 1959), pp. 169-171.
FRAZIER, ALEXANDER. "Broadening the Experience of the Culturally Disadvantaged," *ALA Bulletin,* 58 (June 1964), pp. 523-526.
———. "Teaching the Culturally Deprived," *National Elementary Principal,* 4 (February 1963), pp. 16-19.

GOETLIEB, DAVID. "Views of Negro and White Teachers," *Sociology of Education*, 37 (Summer 1964), pp. 345-353.

GROFF, PATRICK. "Dissatisfactions in Teaching the CD Child," *Phi Delta Kappan*, 45 (November 1963), p. 76.

GUILD, JUNE P. "Who Is a Negro?" *Journal of Negro Education*, 35 (Winter 1964), pp. 83-84.

HARRISON, E. C. "Working at Improving the Motivational and Achievement Levels of the Deprived," *Journal of Negro Education*, 32 (Summer 1963), pp. 375-383.

HAVIGHURST, R. J. "Who Are the Culturally Deprived?" *Journal of Negro Education*, 36 (Winter 1965), pp. 39-46.

HAYNES, HARRY. "Language Arts Program for Culturally Deprived," *Schools Journal*, 46 (Spring 1962).

HOBERT, CHARLES. "Underachievement Among Minority Group Students," *Phylon*, 24 (Summer 1963), pp. 184-196.

IRRIG, M. "Developing Character Through Reading," *Wilson Library Bulletin*, 33 (April 1959).

KILLENS, JOHN OLIVER. "Explanation of the 'Black Psyche'," *New York Times Magazine*, Section 6 (June 7, 1964), p. 37.

KOHN, MELVIN L. "Social Class and Parent-Child Relationships: An Interpretation," *American Journal of Sociology*, 68 (July 1963), p. 11.

LLOYD, HELEN. "What's Ahead in Reading for the Disadvantaged?" *The Reading Teacher*, 18 (March 1965).

MAYS, N. "Behavior Expectations of Negro and White Teachers," *Journal of Negro Education*, 32 (Spring 1963), pp. 223-228.

MECKEL, HENRY C. "English and the Non-Academic Student," *California Journal of Secondary Education*, 34 (March 1957), pp. 175-178.

MONROE, RAWLIN. "Race, Illustrations, and Interest Materials for Reading and Creative Writing," *Journal of Negro Education*, 34 (Winter 1964), pp. 232-237.

NEWTON, EUNICE S. "Planning for the Language Development of Disadvantaged Children and Youth," *Journal of Negro Education*, 33 (Summer 1964), pp. 264-276. This article proposes generalizations of verbal disadvantages and suggests ways of helping pupils upgrade their linguistic skills.

OSTRACH, H. F. "English and the Lower Class Student," *English Journal*, 52 (March 1963), pp. 196-199.

RIESSMAN, FRANK, and JEAN GOLDFARB. "Role Playing and the Poor," *Group Psychotherapy*, 17, No. 1, 1964.

ROSS, FRANK. "For the Disadvantaged Student—A Program That Swings," *English Journal*, 54 (April 1965).

SMILEY, MARJORIE. "Gateway English: Teaching English to Disadvantaged Students," *English Journal*, 54 (April 1965).

STOLLEY, RICHARD B. "The Child Seller," *Life* (October 8, 1965), pp. 109-118.

WOLF, RECIA, and FRANK WOLF. "Helping Children Who Do Not Want to Learn," *Journal of Educational Sociology*, 29 (October 1955), pp. 89-96.

ZAMCHICK, DAVID. "The Battle of the Book: Slow Learners," *Clearing House*, 33 (September 1958), pp. 41-43.

MATERIALS FOR TEACHERS

Bulletin of Education, **20** (Spring 1966). Lawrence, Kan.: University of Kansas, School of Education. Reports on current problems in educating the disadvantaged. Paul C. Burns presents a thorough review in his article, "Language Arts Methods and Materials for the Disadvantaged Youth," pp. 113-122.

BURNS, PAUL C., and ROBERT W. RIDGWAY. *Diagnosing Reading Difficulties Through Classroom Procedures.* Boston: Ginn and Company, Contributions in Reading, No. 30.

CROSBY, MURIEL, and an N.C.T.E. committee. *Reading Ladders for Human Relations.* Champaign, Ill.: National Council of Teachers of English, 0000.

DAVIS, ALLISON. "Society, the School, and the Student," *Improving English Skills of Culturally Different Youth.* Office of Education Bulletin No. 5. Washington, D.C.: U.S. Department of Health, Education, and Welfare, 1964, p. 21.

Department of Secondary School Principals Bulletin, Vol. 47 (March 1963). Washington, D.C.: NEA. Contains such articles as "Program for Individual Differences," "A Junior High School Course for Disadvantaged Students," "Replications of Some Aspects of Higher Horizons Program in a Southern Junior High School," "Working with the Underachieving Students."

DUNN, ANITE E., MABEL E. JACKMAN, and J. ROY NEWTON. *Fare for the Reluctant Reader.* Albany, N.Y.: Capital Area School Development Association, State University of New York, 1965.

"Educational Planning for Socially Disadvantaged Children and Youth," *Journal of Negro Education,* Yearbook, **33** (Summer 1964), pp. 203-366. Contains articles by Martin Deutsch, Robert Havighurst, Harold Spears, Carl Marburger, and Goodwin Watson.

EMERY, RAYMOND C., and MARGARET B. HOUSHOWER. *High Interest—Easy Reading for Junior and Senior High School Reluctant Readers.* Champaign, Ill.: National Council of Teachers of English, 1965.

GUILFOILE, ELIZABETH. *Books for Beginning Readers.* Champaign, Ill.: National Council for Teachers of English, 1963.

Illinois State University Journal, **28** (December 1965). Normal, Ill.: Illinois State University Press. Entire issue is devoted to various problems of teaching and evaluating the disadvantaged student.

Literature Sampler. Chicago, Ill.: Learning Materials, Inc. The *Literature Sampler* is a very attractive collection of verbatim excerpts from a wide variety of action-filled stories at seven different reading levels and in ten interest areas: adventure, mystery, humor, success, sports, science and science fiction, animals, rebellion, people, and the teen-age world.

Paper Bound Books in Print. New York: R. R. Bowker Co., 1967.

Phi Delta Kappan, **45** (November 1963). Bloomington, Ill.: Phi Delta Kappan. Contains such articles as "Issues in Educating the Culturally Disadvantaged," "Dissatisfactions in Teaching the CD Child," "Alienated Youth

Here and Abroad," "Educating Culturally Deprived Youth in Urban Centers."

Reader's Choice. New York: Scholastic Book Services, 1966.

RUSSELL, DAVID. *Listening Aids Through the Grades*. New York: Bureau of Publications, Columbia University, 1952. Presents a specific collection of listening games and exercises, and suggests practical ideas and activities for the teaching of listening.

Scholastic Literature Units. New York: Scholastic Book Services, 1966. Scholastic literature units for grades 7, 8, 9, and 10 include a paperback anthology of 20 short selections plus a wide variety of paperbacks to spark the reader's interest and to match his ability. Reading placement tests, guides, and other practical classroom aids are included.

SPACHE, GEORGE D. *Good Reading for Poor Readers*. Champaign, Ill.: Garrard Press, 1963. Valuable collection of high-interest, low-level vocabulary reading materials.

STRANG, RUTH, ETHELYNE PHELPS, and DOROTHY WITHROW. *Gateways to Readable Books*. New York: H. W. Wilson Company, 1958.

SULLIVAN, HELEN BLAIR, and LORRAINE E. TOLMAN. *High Interest-Low Vocabulary Reading Material*. Boston: Boston University School of Education, 1961.

Supplement to Teaching Guide for Language Arts, Grades 1-12. Chicago, Ill.: Bureau of Curriculum Development. Includes reading, listening, speaking, and writing skills for the culturally different.

The Paperback Goes to School. New York: Bureau of Independent Publishers and Distributers, 1962.

WATTENBERG, WILLIAM W. "Education for the Culturally Deprived," *National Elementary Principal*, 44 (November 1964), pp. 16-19. This issue contains five articles on educating the culturally deprived.

Your Reading. Champaign, Ill.: National Council of Teachers of English, 1960.

MATERIALS FOR STUDENTS

ANDERSON, LORENA, *et al. Listen and Read Tapes*. Huntington, N.Y.: Educational Developmental Laboratories, 1963. Recordings of poetry, short stories, dramatizations, and choral readings used to develop appreciation and better listening skills. Set of 30 in a file box—Set G-L, levels 7-12.

ALLEN, ROBERT L., and VIRGINIA F. ALLEN. *Read Along with Me*. New York: Bureau of Publications, Teachers College, Columbia University, 1964. Presents a modified phonics approach to beginning reading instruction incorporating the interesting device of reading along by teacher and pupil. Includes manual, booklet on rhyming words, and booklet of stories.

Education, 85 (April 1965). Indianapolis, Ind.: Bobbs-Merrill Company, Inc. Contains such articles as "Materials and Methods in Reading," "Purposeful Language Arts Program," and "Broadening the Experiences of Deprived Readers."

Educational Leadership, 20 (February 1963). Washington, D.C.: Association for Supervision and Curriculum Development. Contains such articles as

"The Drop-Out—Our Greatest Challenge," "Guidance for the Disaf-
fected," "If Johnny Doesn't Care. . . .," "Pupils Who Do Not Respond."
English Journal, **54** (April 1965). Champaign, Ill.: National Council of Teachers of English. Carries a number of articles focusing on the teaching of
English to the disadvantaged child in America.

FROSTIG, MARRIANNE, and DAVID HORNE. *The Frostig Program for Development
of Visual Perception.* Chicago: Follett Publishing Company, 1964. Intended
as a prereading program emphasizing development of visual perception
(position in space, spatial relationships; perceptual constancy, visual-motor
coordination, and figure ground perception). Complete set includes 359
ditto masters for worksheets.

HERBER, HAROLD L. *Learning Your Language/One.* Chicago: Follett Publishing Company, 1964. Suggested for elementary and junior high school slow
learners. Six different booklets and a teacher's guide.

HOOK, J. N., and WILLIAM H. EVANS. *Individualized English.* Chicago: Follett
Publishing Company, 1964. Programmed instruction for junior high school
years. Set can be used by about 35 students.

Merrill Palmer Quarterly, **10** (June 1964). Detroit: Merrill Palmer Institute.
Carries articles focuing on the teaching of the disadvantaged student.

MILLER, WARD S. *Word Wealth*, and *Word Wealth Junior.* New York: Holt,
Rinehart, and Winston, Inc. (With Teachers Manual for *Word Wealth
Junior.*)

MOORE, ROBERT W. *Effective Writing.* New York: Holt, Rinehart, and Winston, Inc., 1965.

POSTMAN, NEIL, and HOWARD C. DAMON. *The Uses of Language.* New York:
Holt, Rinehart, and Winston, Inc., 1965.

———. *Language and Systems.* New York: Holt, Rinehart, and Winston, Inc.,
1965.

———.*The Language of Discovery.* New York: Holt, Rinehart, and Winston,
Inc., 1965.

RICHARDSON, JACK E., JR., H. E. SMITH, Jr., and B. J. WEISS. *It Happens on a
Ranch.* New York: Harper and Row, Publishers, 1965. (*The Linguistic
Readers, A Basic Program/First Reader.*)

SHEHAN, LAWRENCE P. *English and You*, with Teacher's Manual and Answer
Book; *English Can Be Easy*, with Teacher's Manual and Answer Book;
English for Americans, with Teacher's Manual and Answer Book. New
York: Holt, Rinehart, and Winston, Inc.

The National Elementary Principal, **44** (November 1964). Washington, D.C.:
NEA. Includes such articles as "Leadership in Schools Serving the Educationally Disadvantaged," and "An Approach to the Problems of a Down-
town School."

The Reading Teacher, **18** (March 1965). Pittsburgh, Pa.: International Reading
Association. Contains such articles as "What's Ahead in Reading for the
Disadvantaged?" "Upgrading Instruction Through Special Reading Services," "After-School Study Centers in New York City," "In-Service Training of Teachers to Work with the Disadvantaged."

TINCHER, ETHEL, *et al. Success in Language/A.* Chicago: Follett Publishing

Company, 1964. For secondary school slow learners. (Six different booklets and a teacher's guide.)

TURNER, RICHARD H. *The Turner-Livingston Reading Series.* Chicago: Follett Publishing Company, 1964. Includes the following titles: "The Money You Spend"; "The Town You Live In"; "The Jobs You Get"; "The Person You Are"; "The Friends You Make"; "The Family You Belong to." The reading level is relatively low; the content is appropriate. For junior high school level.

———. *The Turner-Livingston Communication Series.* Chicago: Follett Publishing Company, 1965. Includes the following titles: "The Television You Watch"; "The Phone Calls You Make"; "The Newspaper You Read"; "The Movies You See"; "The Letters You Write"; "The Language You Speak." The style is appropriate to the content. For junior high school level.

———. *When People Talk on the Telephone.* New York: Bureau of Publications, Teachers College, Columbia University, 1964. Depicts real situations requiring telephone communication in language appropriate to the socially mature but backward reader. The vignettes are convincing; the participants are of all races and backgrounds; the content is derived from the cultures of various subgroups. For junior high school level.

FILMS AND FILMSTRIPS

Broken Mask (29 min. b/w, BFC, rental). Hidden roots of prejudice explored when deeds had to replace words in race relations.

Burden of Truth (43 or 67 min., ADL). Explosion of stereotypical myths about minority groups.

Cast the First Stone (42 min. b/w, ADL). Explores the psychology of prejudice in all groups.

Detached American (33 min. c, PSU). Responsibility and involvement in the "no-man-is-an-island" theme.

Down in the Street (52 min. b/w, PSU, 1960). Neighborhood conditions in the Negro ghetto and their social implications.

Free to be Different (50 frames, ADL). Role of plurality in American culture; "melting pot" concept.

Harlem Crusaders (29 min. b/w, PSU, 1962). Struggle for survival in gangs and social worker's role in setting value tones.

High Lonesome Sound (30 min. b/w, PSU, 1963). Aloneness of minority in "other" culture.

In White America (60 min. b/w, TIO, rental). Discrepancy between stated and behavioral values via dramatic scenes by popular actors.

Joe Davis, American (13 min. b/w, AFL-CIO). Contributions of Negro minority to American culture.

Let's Live Democracy (18 min. 37 frames, PFC). Details some of the rights professed for minorities and their rationale. (E1)

Man—One Family (57 frames, PFC). Common attributes of mankind which make all men brothers.

Neighborhoods Are Different (11 min. b/w, PSU). Study of the urban sprawl and its consequences as a function of real-estate restrictions.

None So Blind (57 frames, ADL, PFC). Explores the smugness of Americans toward minorities and ultimately the world.

Our Friendly Neighbor (EAV). Nine strips on all phases of Mexican life. Mexican contributions (Spanish implied) to American Culture. (E1)

Portrait of a Disadvantaged Child (16 min. c, PSU). Poverty and value systems of the poor Negro and poor white explored. (E1)

Portrait of the Inner City (17 min. c, PSU). Effects of neighborhood blight on value systems of residents' children. (E1)

Portrait of the Inner City School: a Place to Learn (19 min. c, PSU). Conflict in value systems between middle-class schools and disadvantaged students. (E1)

Teaching Slow Learners (30 min. b/w, FPC, free for viewing). Describes typical daily lesson and methodology for slow learners. Though World History is the focus, content and method apply to English.

The Challenge (30 min. b/w, ADL). Exploration of the moral fiber behind the American belief in equal rights.

The Forty Sounds of English (40 min. b/w, ITA). Shows the use of initial teaching alphabet approach to reading instruction.

The Spiral of Social Change (44 frames, ADL, PFC). Presents the historical need for tolerance and flexibility for survival.

To Live Together (35 min. b/w, ADL, PFC). One-world theme explored through the rationale for tolerance.

The Loon's Necklace (12 min. c, PSU). Cartoon-like exploration of tolerance for religious beliefs. (E1)

The New Girl (30 min. b/w, ADL). Adjustment problems faced by the first Negro to break the racial barrier in an all white school.

Walk to Freedom (20 min. b/w, AFSC). Freedom marchers in the deep South and their objectives.

We Live in Peace (60 frames, ADL). Plea for tolerance of other cultures and nations by stressing their contributions.

TAPES AND RECORDS

Anthology of Negro Poets (EAV, record). Negro perceptions of life and liberty in "Mr. Charlie's" world.

Heart of Darkness (NCTE, record). Moving presentation of Conrad's exploration of intolerance.

In White America (Columbia records). Excerpts from plays, poems, and stories which comment ironically on prejudice.

James Baldwin (EAV, record). Mr. Baldwin reads excerpts from his essays and stories about the contemporary Negro.

John Brown's Body (EAV, record). Dramatic quartet presents S. V. Benet's views on Northern and Southern views of the Negro.

Least Successful Lessons (Hunter College, N.Y.). Describes lessons on grooming, reading, social studies, letter writing, arithmetic, and poetry. (Tape)

Mark Twain's Mississippi (EAV, record). Excerpts from Twain's writings—
social satires of hypocritical whites.

Mark Twain on the Damned Human Race (EAV, record). Bitter condemna-
tion of prejudice of all sorts, particularly as learned through religion.

Most Successful Lessons (Hunter College, N.Y.). Describes a lesson in English
composition, spelling, social studies, art, courtesy, creative writing, and
arithmetic. (Tape)

Tennessee Williams (NCTE, record). Williams' subtle examination of the
roots of Southerners' prejudices.

Wilfredo (Hunter College, N.Y.). Tells of work over a period of time with a
"difficult" child. (Tape)

William Faulkner (NCTE, record). Castigation of Southern smugness and
decadence, especially toward the Negro.

The First Day (Hunter College, N.Y.). Tells of the first day in learning to
teach in difficult schools. (Tape)

DISTRIBUTORS

ADL: Anti-Defamation League of B'nai Brith, 225 South 15th Street, Philadelphia, Pa. 19102.

AFL-CIO: American Federation of Labor and Congress of Industrial Organizations, Film Division, Department of Education, 815 Sixteenth Street,
N.W., Washington, D.C. 20206.

AFSC: American Friends Service Committee, Community Relations Program,
160 North 15th Street, Philadelphia, Pa. 19102.

BFS: Broadcasting and Film Commission, National Council of Churches of
Christ in the U.S.A., 220 Fifth Avenue, New York, N.Y. 10001.

EAV: Educational Audio-Visual, Inc., 29 Maple Avenue, Pleasantville, N.Y.
10570.

FPC: Follett Publishing Company, 1257 South Wabash Avenue, Chicago, Ill.
60607.

ITA: Initial Teaching Alphabet Productions, 20 East 46th Street, New York,
N.Y. 10017.

NCTE: National Council of Teachers of English, 508 South Sixth Street,
Champaign, Ill. 61822.

PFC: Philadelphia Fellowship Commission, Community Services Department,
225 South 15th Street, Philadelphia, Pa. 19102.

PSU: Pennsylvania State Audio-Visual Service, Room 3 Pattee Library, University Park, Pa. 16802.

TIO: Television Information Office, 666 Fifth Avenue, New York, N.Y. 10019.

INDEX

New teaching techniques, attitudes, and methods courses are explored in this new approach to more effective English and reading courses for disadvantaged youth. It is intended for use as a textbook in elementary and secondary education courses, as a reference for English and reading teachers, and for NDEA institutes for in-service programs.

The ideas of the contributors were tested in a 1965 NDEA institute; the book's material has been accumulated from field studies, research and personal experiences of educators in the field.

Each article is prefaced by an introduction describing the nature of the article. The addition of reference and material sources—films, tapes, etc.— organized by medium, provides the student with resources for executing the techniques developed in the text. These additional features enhance the author's intent to direct the future junior-senior high school teacher toward enlightened attitudes in this sensitive area of education.

The authors' use of research and institute materials was tested in the Bellefonte, Pa. area, among junior-senior high school students from non-urban backgrounds.